How To Raise A Dog When Nobody's Home

◆————————————◆

Complete Training for the Family Dog

◆————————————◆

Second Edition

By Jerry Climer
Illustrated by Mary Jung

Set in typeface designed for easy reading.
Printed in the United States of America

Library of Congress Cataloging in Publication Data
International Standard Book Number 0-911793-03-8

Penny Dreadful Publishers
315 S. Bowen St., PO Box 364
Jackson, Michigan 49203

Preface

Dear Readers,

In this book I have tried to share with you the joy and companionship I have had with my dogs and the rewards of having well-trained, fun-loving canine friends.

I designed the book to be read from cover to cover in just a few evenings. Along with training tips there are also stories, legends, and tales to instruct and entertain you.

Once you have read this easy-to-use guide to successful dog training, you will wish to refer to it frequently as you encounter discipline problems with your growing pup. In fact, you will notice that many times the solutions given in one area of training, may also be used successfully in other situations.

I hope all of you from eight to eighty enjoy raising a healthy, happy, loving dog to maturity and old age with the help of this book.

Jerry Climer

To my delightful family,
Jim, children and pets who
push lovingly when I falter

With special appreciation:
Juanita Riedel
Lisa Climer Harding
Marian Koppler

Alfred J. Bruey for
his poem
A Day in the Life of Lassie

CONTENTS

Part 1

How To Raise A Dog When Nobody's Home

Today's pets have a new lifestyle 3
A wake-up massage 4
Window watching 5
Stimulating surprises 6
Early training prevents poor adult behavior 6
Most biters are house pets 7
Nip that nippin' early 9
Puppy's first lesson 9
Please fence me in 12
Teaching puppy to stay alone 15
The growing puppy 16
Evening training 17
Housebreaking the dog 19
Gnawing and chewing 22
Socialize the shy dog 25
Teach the game of "come when called" 26
Building vocabulary 29
Teaching puppy "come" out of doors 29
"Come" "sit" "stay" 31

Dog collars—fashionable and practical 34
Walking together 37
Heeling on leash 37
No jumping 39
Jumping by invitation 40
Talk to animals with key words 41
Teaching your dog to ride in auto 44
Libra and the car 46
Insist your dog uses good manners 48
Keep your dog cool 49
Practice, patience and praise 51

Part 2

Nobody's Home Dog Grows Up

Dog's purpose on earth 57
Communication—key to successful training 58
"Down" "Stay" 60
Obedience class 61
Carrie and Kilty 63
Puppy wetting 66
Inner determination 68
How to make a nylon pull toy 70
Good dogs are made, not born 73
Acceptable chew toys 74
Chewing—different discipline for older dogs 75

Training with balloons 77
Balloons as imaginative deterrents 79
There's a trick to "sit up" training 80
"Come when called"—for your growing dog 84
Cricket the terrible 85
Clever pets can talk 87
Plants and pets 89
"Take" "hold" "give" 92
Smart dogs "carry" 93
"Fetch the paper" 95
"On your rug" 96
Control dog's barking 98
Firm discipline stops barking 99
Pack animals need leadership 101
Classy tricks for classy dogs 101
Practice, patience, praise teaches trick 103
Pets can have emotional problems 104
New baby in the home 105
Help for the frustrated pet 106

Part 3

Home Health Care

The story of St. Roch and his dog 111
That skillful intruder—the common flea 112
Even "best friend" needs a bath 117
Trimming your dog's nails 119
Care of the ears 121
Shopping for a veterinarian 124

Timing crucial for veterinarian 126
Protection from heartworm 130
Cosmetic surgery 132
Psychology of play 134
Playing with your dog 135
Frisbee, catch and fetch 137
The best games for you and your dog 138

Part 4

Man and Dog: Living, Loving and Coping

How the dog got its wet nose 143
Two owners—one dog—a shared experience 143
Cases and cages 146
Happy is the dog whose owner loves to jog 147
Jogging—how to cope with stray dogs 149
Domestic and overseas traveling 151
Vacation safety tips 152
Hot diggity dog—but not in the garden 154
Introducing second dog is touchy 156
Finding a new home for your pet 160
A Day in the Life of Lassie by Alfred J. Bruey 162
Index 163

INTRODUCTION

In more than 65 percent of the homes in America today, the wife as well as the husband leaves the house or apartment each morning for at least eight hours of work. At the same time, the children depart for school or the babysitter.

This daily mass exodus of the family leaves a large percentage of the 45 to 50 million dogs living in the United States to fend for themselves.

Whether the dog lives in the lap of luxury or the poorest of homes, trouble begins when this most sociable of all animals is confined to loneliness and boredom without advance preparation.

Due to the changing patterns in American living, it is time for dog writers and trainers to become realistic and talk about "How to raise a dog when nobody's home."

Part 1

How To Raise A Dog When Nobody's Home

TODAY'S PETS HAVE A NEW LIFESTYLE

Having grown up with dogs, it took me many years as an adult to realize that a home with children and family around all day is an exciting, stimulating environment for any household pet. Living happily each day and getting plenty of exercise with the family, our pets were rarely overweight or depressed.

Today's home environment has changed drastically from a decade ago. The majority of homes are vacated each morning, as parents and children go off to work, school, or the baby-sitter. Where our pets used to have school children return to the home in the early afternoon, the family now returns together, often no sooner than dinnertime, during many months of the year.

3

This means that the family exits the house in darkness and returns in darkness. Since our pets judge their day by natural light, their best hours are now spent alone in an empty house or apartment.

I do not in any way believe that you can completely change a canine's biological time clock. However, I do leave a light burning to dispel the darkness. Dogs see well in semi-darkness and most of them remain in wakeful attentiveness, even while half-dozing during the night.

AVOIDING DEPRESSION: With the absence of their loved ones, confined within the same overly familiar floors and walls, boredom becomes the norm and soon depression sets in. When depressed, just as humans, pets will overeat and become overweight.

Having worked with this problem, which worries all absentee pet owners who love their pets, I have come up with a routine which my dogs and I enjoy. And—they stay in top form, both mentally and physically.

The reason my pets are happy to rest contentedly during the night is that I give them enough stimulation during the early evening hours to at least tire the darlings.

A WAKE-UP MASSAGE

Basically, all I am doing from the time I return home until bedtime is help the dogs adapt to a few hour's change in their schedule. This makes their life a little more interesting and, of course, this activity makes my pets more interesting to me.

When I say I massage my dogs each evening upon returning home, I use the word to denote a firm, playful roughing up of the coat, scratching the ears, throat and tummy, and pulling on the legs and tail. At the same time, I tell them how much I've missed their happy faces. You could use a firm bristle or wire slicker brush to produce a similar stimulant.

There is no preferred procedure for this, since it is done to increase the canine's circulation up to normal after a period of rest. Any hands-on method of massage that you and your dogs enjoy to produce the following results are acceptable. Within minutes, you will notice an added sparkle to your pet's eyes and he will become alert, active, and ready for fun.

If your dogs are sleepy and inactive during the evening as mine used to be, you will be delighted with this new, happy, alert pet who wants to share your precious hours with fun and affection.

WINDOW WATCHING

A window is a very important possession for indoor pets, and if at all possible, they should have access to the exciting view of their world. Many of my dogs' hours are spent sitting comfortably near their window watching the world go by and hoping to spot another dog. When an intruder is seen, confusion reigns, as both housebound pets run from window to window, barking in blissful excitement. If you cannot provide a window, a well-covered tank with active fish will also give occasional entertainment.

STIMULATING SURPRISES

Of course, my dogs still sleep some during the day, but with an assortment of toys which are circulated almost daily, life is at least interesting to them. Sleeping and eating then does not become the primary function of the day.

While I prefer not to leave food for the dogs during the day, there are frequent treats and surprises. We have one lower cupboard which their big noses are able to open. Often they find a much-loved snack or a different toy to carry about the house.

Sometimes I observe my dogs playing "King of the Mountain," as one pet refuses to allow the other inside the magic hiding place. Such activities provide mental stimulation and physical exertion. Isn't this exactly what we wish our dogs to be—alert, active, and sociable companions?

EARLY TRAINING PREVENTS POOR ADULT BEHAVIOR

Let's talk about you and me. We are the typical owners of an average puppy. Consider our mental and physical condition when coming home tired and hungry after a day of work or play. We certainly are not in the mood to discipline and train our dog. We might have been willing to give the pup some love and attention and even played a bit if we hadn't found that puppy had misbehaved while left alone. When this happens all hell breaks loose. We yell and hit; the dog cringes and sulks. The evening is ruined.

This kind of situation can be prevented when we realize that almost all serious behavior problems in growing puppies can be avoided. The whole trick is knowing what to do and when to do it.

It's a fact that many serious behavior problems in growing dogs don't develop until the age of six months or older. Destructive chewing, digging, biting, barking and soiling by dogs six months or older is a direct result of poor puppy training. *Bad habits can be prevented.*

MOST BITERS ARE HOUSE PETS

The U.S. Disease Control Center in Atlanta, Georgia estimates that about one million people in the United States are bitten by dogs every year. A majority of victims are children between the ages of five and eight. Most of the biting dogs are house pets.

This is no surprise to me since I repeatedly hear dog owners defend their spoiled dogs, saying "He only bit because he was protecting his food," or "He was startled." The most exasperating excuse is "It was only a small puncture, so we didn't have to go to the doctor."

Over 90 percent of all dog bites occur within the family, or to friends of the dog's owner. Three out of ten bites to youngsters under ten are on the face where the greatest threat of injury and disfigurement exists.

Need I say more! Can anyone possibly excuse a dog for biting? The only reason I could excuse him is when there is a real and definite threat to the dog owner's life or property.

Many dogs will bite if provoked enough. Any dog can develop into a biter if he is not properly trained. Growling, snarling and nipping are sure indications of a bite to come, if the dog is not corrected immediately.

Dogs fear many of the same things that people fear: a stranger on their property, loss of possessions such as food or toys, threats to their loved ones and harsh punishment. People show hostility and anger with words; dogs use their mouths. Sometimes dogs only bark, but unless taught otherwise, they also will bite.

Biting is a symptom of the fears and anxieties a dog feels. Affection and proper training, while a dog is still young, will relieve anxiety and allow the pup to grow up happy, outgoing and friendly.

Proper training never makes a dog less protective. Just the opposite is true. A happy, friendly dog relieved of fears will be able to distinguish friend from foe without hesitation.

NIP THAT NIPPIN' EARLY

The most secure time in a dog's life is while he is a pup, living in the small world of a loving mother and littermates. The outside world is unknown at this time and in the narrow confines of the home, all is love and happiness.

By the time the puppy is six to eight weeks old, the situation changes and a new home is found. Suddenly the pup is removed from the loving mother and is forced to adjust to a totally new environment and family.

Animal psychologists say this is one of the most important times in a pup's life. If at the time of change to new surroundings the pup does not get love, attention, fondling and reassurance, he will grow up fearful and full of anxiety.

Dogs bite, nip or snap when fearful or angry. To prevent these problems later in life, teach your pup to be tolerant and friendly. Remember, he received a great deal of discipline from his wise mother before he left the litter. You are just continuing his mother's training.

PUPPY'S FIRST LESSON

One of the earliest lessons your puppy should learn is never to wiggle, squirm or nip when picked up or held. Even a pup who will be too big to pick up when full grown must learn this lesson. There will be many times in the dog's life when he will have to be picked up, handled or examined. He must learn to accept it patiently, without anger.

To start this lesson, sit on the floor and pick up your puppy. Until your pup learns to stay quiet when held, always insist that he be kept close to the floor. This prevents injury if the pup suddenly jumps from your arms.

While holding the pup, speak soothing, affectionate words to him, but hold him firmly. Tuck the pup's back end under your arm with your elbow tight against the dog's outside rear hip. If he is small enough, firmly grasp the front paws with the same hand. This leaves the other hand free to pet or discipline the dog. This hold is a good firm lock and will make the dog feel secure. Any pup, if not held securely, will attempt to free himself because he fears falling.

Some puppies love to be picked up and held; others wiggle, lunge and mouth your hand to escape. If not taught to endure being handled and examined while young, a headstrong pup will snap at anyone, including his owner or veterinarian, later in life.

Sit on the floor and pick up your puppy. When he struggles to free himself speak soothingly and pet his head to calm him. If he does not quiet down, give him a little shake and firmly say "no."

When he tries to nip or mouth your hand, hold his mouth closed for a few seconds, say "no," then release. While you are holding the pup, open his mouth and examine his teeth. Many times in his life he will have his mouth examined. By starting now, he will accept mouth examinations later with no fear.

The minute the pup becomes quiet and accepts your handling, praise him. Remember: Always praise your dog as soon as he obeys you.

All early discipline is done gently but firmly because you are training a very young puppy. If this lesson is taught later in the dog's life you will have to be more firm. In fact, you may have to wear gloves to prevent being bitten.

Some puppies will lie quietly in your arms from the first time they are picked up. If your pup remains calm, give him praise and affection, and put him carefully back on the floor. With this pup you will probably have no problems. However, it is still a good idea to pick him up occasionally and run your hands over his body to be sure he will continue to enjoy being touched as he grows. It's also helpful to occasionally allow other people to hold the puppy while he is young.

Teaching your puppy to endure handling will take only a few minutes of your time, twice a day. During these few minutes you have taught your dog:

You are his leader.
He must learn patience and self-control.
Even when provoked, he may not use his teeth.
The hand that loves will also discipline.

PLEASE FENCE ME IN

For your own peace of mind, it is essential that you have an area, room or cage to put your dog into while you are busy or away from home. You must feel that puppy is safe, comfortable and out of mischief. Until the pup is completely toilet trained, newspapers should be kept on the floor of the area. Also provide fresh drinking water in a heavy bowl (I like pottery). Toys for chewing are also important and will be discussed later.

Be sure that there is nothing within the area that will injure the puppy, and clear this section of anything your dog could hurt or destroy. If there is some object in the pen that you cannot remove (I had a built-in desk), dab Tabasco sauce on the wood. Don't worry, the hot sauce won't hurt the pup but it will discourage chewing.

Dog psychologists agree that puppies feel more secure in a reasonably small enclosed area. The warmth of a small pen reminds him of mother's nest. This is the reason you will find that almost all kitchens are too large to allow the pup freedom; and at the other extreme, most cages that are bought are too soon outgrown to warrant the high cost of purchase.

We found the ideal solution when my husband Jim spent less than $20.00 to build a room divider with a hinged gate at the end of our kitchen. We had the barricade built and the pen completely ready before we took our Standard Poodle, Libra, from the kennel.

A. ⅜" PLYWOOD
B. SCREEN ON
   1" x 2" FRAME
C. HOOK & EYE

The divider included a wood panel connected to a gate with hinges. The panel slipped between the cupboard and the refrigerator. The gate was about four feet high since Libra was destined to become a large Standard Poodle. Screening used in the gate gave the dog an excellent view of the family activities at all times.

When you build your own dog pen or room divider, you will have to decide the height of your dog's lodgings by the adult size your dog will become.

I used the dog pen until Libra was completely housebroken and obedience trained enough to behave while having the run of the house for at least eight hours. Of course the older Libra became, the less it was necessary to use the dog pen. She was about eight months old when we finally removed the divider. By that time I expected Libra to behave when company called, and go to her rug when told. Her rug was placed in the area where her pen had been and to this day Libra considers this her special corner. She was expected to wait to relieve herself out of doors, stay off the furniture, chew only on her toys, and in general behave like a well-trained dog.

Any reasonably small area is sufficient for limited confinement of your puppy as long as you don't expect him to stay in the pen constantly.

I am assuming that you will give your pup lots of love, fun, attention and exercise, along with consistent discipline. This is the formula for raising a well-adjusted, friendly, alert, out-going pup that will love and protect you and your property.

I must add a word of caution about housing a dog out of doors. Years ago almost all dogs were raised out of doors. Today there is no place that a dog can be safe when left out of doors without constant supervision. All you have to do is read the newspapers with their tales of animal abuse to know what I mean.

When you are away from home, the only place you can be assured of keeping your dog safe is either with you, or in a locked house.

I don't like the idea of leaving a puppy in the basement or garage. Since he cannot see or hear in such complete isolation, he will become lonely and bored. This can lead to poor toilet training, destructive behavior and either a nervous snapping dog, or a shy, frightened canine who cowers at his shadow.

14

Dogs, like all living creatures, need love and sunshine in which to bask and grow.

TEACHING PUPPY TO STAY ALONE

Teaching puppy to stay alone for an eight-hour day is an absolute must for today's busy people. Since your puppy's first learning experience begins the moment he enters your home, working people will find that it is easiest to bring puppy home at the start of a weekend.

Puppy's first lesson will be to stay quietly in his pen until you decide he may leave.

Since your pup has been with his littermates until now, he will certainly feel lonesome for a short time. It will be difficult, but necessary for you to resist your puppy's cries and baby antics to get his own way. In fact, it will be necessary for you to harden your heart and begin some gentle, but firm, discipline.

The easiest method of teaching puppy to enjoy his pen and stay alone without protest is to sit in the pen with him occasionally for the first few days. This will reassure him that he will not be ignored in his pen and it might even be a pleasant place to stay. Everyone in your household will want to give the new dog some attention and there is no safer place than the pen with papers on the floor.

Go in and out of the pen as often as you wish, but firmly push the puppy back and close the gate as you leave. When your dog is quiet, praise him; if he barks or whines, tell him "no" in a firm voice. *Never allow your puppy out of his pen when he is noisy or barking.*

If you have told your pup "no" and he continues to be noisy, slap a rolled newspaper on your open hand while repeating "no." The noise will startle and distract the pup long enough for you to praise his silence.

With consistent discipline, your puppy will be quite content in his pen and remain quiet until you return home. The toys, bones and balls you leave in his pen will help him to pass the time happily anticipating the fun to come at the end of the day.

THE GROWING PUPPY

When you have a puppy under five months old, and you are away all day, it will be necessary for you to come home for lunch. Any pup this young needs to be put outside to relieve himself at this time. He also needs a little love and attention and a chance to exercise. If coming home at noon is impossible for you, try to find a neighbor or relative to take care of the dog.

Coming home at noon may be a hardship, but it will only be for a few months and is extremely important for you and your dog. The dog will soon adjust to your schedule and stay clean until taken out of doors at noon and again in the evening. He will also learn to be patient and good, but only if you do not expect too much, too soon. No one should expect a puppy to stay alone for a full eight-hour day. You would be defeating yourself and discouraging your dog.

With your dog securely confined in a pen, and you and your pup on a workable schedule, life becomes brighter. Upon returning home in the evening, even though tired and hungry, you will be able to greet your dog with loving affection. So what if he did have an accident and soil in his pen. After putting the dog outside, all you have to do is put clean papers in the pen. Now you can relax and enjoy the pup for awhile before starting dinner. The puppy will not be unhappy if he is again put into his pen while dinner is being prepared and eaten, as long as he can see and hear you.

EVENING TRAINING

Another small problem occurs after dinner. You are tired and would like to sit down, read the paper and relax. Puppy, having slept all day, has another idea and soon howls about being left alone in his pen.

If you let the dog loose, he might have an accident on the living room carpet. If left in the pen, the pup will continue to cry and you will feel either guilty or angry.

This is the time to purchase an inexpensive dog collar. Remember, the pup will outgrow it rapidly. Tie a four or five foot piece of twine or rope to the collar and let the puppy drag the lightweight rope around the house. He'll soon be used to the collar and not even notice the rope which is following.

Do not leave the rope on your pup when you are not at home. Puppies can get into the darnedest situations and your pup might harm himself.

With the short rope tied to the pup's collar, you can allow the dog into the living area while still keeping control over his movements. Tie the rope to the leg of your chair, table, or even your ankle, then relax, watch television, or read. At the same time you can keep an eye on the pup to be sure that he doesn't misbehave. You can also talk, pet and play with the pup for awhile before he settles down for another of his frequent naps.

You will be amazed to find how much you will enjoy raising your puppy with the aid of a training rope. From now on you can allow your dog to accompany you around the house and not worry that he will run into a corner to soil the rug, or chew on a forbidden treasure. In return, the puppy will be delighted that he can be with you and will learn good behavior through your firm, loving discipline.

HOUSEBREAKING THE DOG

Housebreaking a puppy can be successfully and quickly accomplished, if you work consistently for a short time.

Dogs and cats are among the few animals which can be housetrained. This is because they are den animals. Wolves, foxes and wild dogs do not soil their living quarters. Horses, birds and other animals live in the open and therefore have no natural desire to live in clean surroundings.

Add to a dog's natural desire to be clean, his desire to please his master, and you can see that any young puppy will become toilet trained as soon as he understands what is expected of him.

Once again the lightweight rope tied to the puppy's collar is of great help. The rope will keep the pup under control any time he is not in his pen.

As you take the dog out to the yard, tell him he is going outside. Stress the word "outside," repeating "outside" every time you go out. Later he will tell you when he wants to go "outside," by lying beside the door or barking. When you take your dog out, go to the same area of the yard each time. This will be a convenience for you, and the pup can learn to use one corner of the yard with no extra training.

Tell puppy to "use your paper" in his special place while out of doors and praise him when he has performed. It's important that you use the same words at all times while training your puppy and always praise him lavishly. As soon as you have praised puppy take him inside immediately to reinforce his outside performance.

Once puppy has performed outside, he must be taken "inside" the house. If you wish to take the pup back outside, remain inside for a few minutes then go back out of doors.

It's important that you never just "put the pup out." This would defeat your purpose, as he must receive praise as well as instruction to know which behavior is correct.

You must always take your dog to his spot and urge him to "use your paper." When he does, always compliment the puppy to show your approval.

Many people think that their puppy will get sick if he is put outside in cold or rainy weather. Unless the pup is a very small toy breed, or in poor health, you need not worry. Puppies have warm coats by the time they leave the litter and can take cold weather better than mere mortals. In fact, the puppy might perform faster outside if he is anxious to get out of the snow or rain.

When your puppy has an accident inside the house, pick him up and firmly say "no, outside," and immediately take him out the door. Once out of doors, again tell pup to "use your paper." At this time, you need not stay out of doors long as the pup only needs to have the idea reinforced by the correction you have just made. Puppy should not be yelled at or hit. *Training takes patience, practice and praise.*

Promptly clean up any accident inside your home. Wash the spot with soap and water several times. It also helps to neutralize the area by applying ammonia and water or vinegar water. Remember that your puppy has a fantastic nose that can smell one part of urine in 60 million parts of water. If he smells urine on a spot in the house, he will likely wet on that spot again if possible. When all else fails, place a chair or footstool over the spot that the dog has wet upon and leave for a few weeks. Hopefully the dog will forget about that area.

Putting yourself and the dog on a schedule for a few weeks will speed up the training process. Take him outside after every meal, then once an hour when you are home and before bedtime. *As my reward for training Kilty and Libra correctly, I can now take the dogs on a trip, stop the car and say "use your paper." Within a few minutes they do their duty, jump back in and away we go.*

Puppies that are alone all day will take a little longer to train but don't give up. Work a little harder on weekends and be consistent with your discipline when you are home.

GNAWING AND CHEWING

Chewing done by dogs can be destructive, dangerous and expensive. Many times it is the most frustrating problem a dog owner encounters. Each year dog lovers lose thousands of dollars worth of property from destructive chewing by their dogs. In addition, many favored pets lose their lives by swallowing poisonous material.

At the very least, chewing by our dogs can ruin a warm and rewarding relationship between dog and master. This often results in a parting of the ways for the unfortunate pet and the angry owner.

Let's look at the problem of destructive chewing and find out what training an owner must do to avoid raising a canine house wrecker.

Mouth development and teeth differ from breed to breed depending on what work the dog was designed to do. All dogs were bred to use their teeth. This desire to chew rarely has any connection with hunger.

Obviously, it is desirable to find out if the dog you just bought or are thinking of buying is known as a destructive house dog. Great Danes, Huskies, Scotties, Dalmations, Old English Sheepdogs and Poodles are not happy when left alone. These dogs will be more inclined to get into mischief if not properly trained.

As we use our hands our dogs use their teeth. Canines will chomp on anything within reach: shoes, furniture, books, rugs, plants, woodwork or the favorite tie you carelessly threw on the chair. A dog must have something to chew on because this is the way it cleans its teeth. If given acceptable toys and at least occasionally a bone or rough dog biscuit you may prevent a great deal of mischief.

My young friend Carl is the proud owner of a new puppy. He knew that if his pup Sitka was going to get into trouble, it probably would occur when the pup was left alone.

One night Carl and his mother, Sandra, left the house, forgetting to lock Sitka in the kitchen. When they returned a short time later, they were appalled to find the living room floor covered with wet dirt from two overturned floor planters.

Sitka had uprooted plants, spilled mud on the carpet and rolled in the dirt.

Of course, for a puppy this was fun. Not so, for Carl and Sandra. They spent the rest of the evening cleaning up the debris and washing the carpet.

To prevent a recurrence and preserve the remaining plants, Sandra used an old training trick which every dog owner should know. She put spots of Tabasco sauce on the planter rim and on some of the leaves.

Tabasco sauce is made of red peppers, vinegar and salt. Since it is used in food for humans, nothing in it will harm a dog. One two-ounce bottle of sauce probably will last through at least two dogs and 50 casseroles of chili.

Hot sauce like Tabasco really works. I have used it for years with every young pup I've trained. It's great to use on electric cords which are dangerous for your dog to chew. You also can use Tabasco on shoes, toys, wood furniture and baseboards, waste baskets and even on book bindings.

When you wish to protect furniture such as sofas and chairs, you may prefer to keep your pup away with a sprinkling of red or black pepper. If you use pepper, it is important that you teach the puppy to dislike the odor.

To do this, sit close to the puppy and sprinkle a small amount of pepper in your hand. Gently blow the pepper very close to the dog's nose. Give him a good whiff and at the same time say "no! bad!" It will take only a few sniffs for the pup to decide that any time he smells pepper he will avoid the place where it is. This works great on rugs, curtains and clothing.

Tabasco, vinegar and either red or black pepper usually are effective on young dogs. If you start while your dog is still a puppy, you may never need stronger discipline.

SOCIALIZE THE SHY DOG

Socialization and basic obedience during the first year of a pup's life should help your pet overcome and control any shy, nervous, or temperamental problems. Exposing him to other people and animals is a beginning step, and many times will quickly improve his behavior. Being assured that other animals and people are fun to be with will increase your dog's self-confidence and develop awareness and a healthy curiosity.

Whenever a dog deviates from its breed characteristics, you must look to the genetic background, or to the past and present environment. When you are aware that you have a problem, you must overcome all trouble by working with the dog's personality and surroundings. If you are alert, as most informed puppy owners are, you will have little difficulty helping your pet while it is young.

Take your pup away from home as often as possible. Allow others to touch and pet the dog while you hold it, or stay near. Walk your canine friend in parks, on city sidewalks, in or near malls, or any place the dog will see other dogs and walkers and learn to enjoy them.

When someone enters your home, bring the pet to meet the visitor. Occasionally allow a friend to give your dog a snack as a small get-acquainted offer. You must be careful about giving too many snacks, even though they are the way to a dog's heart.

When food is used sparingly, it is an excellent training

device. However, many dogs will take advantage of their owners and use good old-fashioned blackmail.

It does take time from your already busy day to socialize your dog, but if it is not done while your puppy is young, you will end up with an unhappy, nervous adult dog that will be difficult to live with. Don't forget, walking a perky pup leads to meeting new friends, sometimes hilarious situations, and excellent muscle conditioning for both you and your best friend.

Remember—your dog will enjoy and learn much more in obedience classes, once you have helped it overcome its handicap.

TEACH THE GAME OF "COME WHEN CALLED"

The story has been told that after God created Adam and all the animals of the earth, a deep gulf opened in the ground, which left Adam on one side of the world and the beasts on the other side. Among the beasts, the dog stood alone gazing at the ever widening gap. Finally in agony at the thought of being separated from his beloved friend, the dog jumped across the gap to stay by the side of man. He has remained there to this day.

I love this legend of dogs' devotion to man. I have always felt that the one way my dogs have shown their devotion to me was to stop whatever they were doing and come when I called. In fact it's a personal insult if my dogs refuse to come. Consequently, I have always started while my pups were very young to teach this lesson.

26

Since canine life is much shorter than human, a dog develops his muscular coordination rapidly. In fact, by the time he is six to eight weeks old, he has good muscular control and is ready to socialize with his human companions. At this time his brain is also ready to learn and his memory will retain his early lessons.

Dog is a creature of habit and learns through constant repetition. The younger you start the lessons of life, the easier it is for both you and the puppy. Since the dog has a natural instinct to chase anything that moves you can start teaching him to "come when called" by playing ball. Puppy will think ball chasing is great fun and both you and your dog will enjoy this learning game.

To start your game, sit on the floor and play with your puppy. When you have his attention, roll the ball across the floor. As you roll the ball tell your dog to "fetch."

The pup will soon run after the ball and pick it up. With coaxing and praise urge him to bring the ball to you. As he starts to return say "Libra come." (Use your own dog's name.)

Each time the puppy brings the ball to you tell him to "give" and remove the ball from his mouth. Now praise him generously and let him know you're sure he's the smartest dog in the world. He wants to please you and will be overjoyed with his great accomplishment.

Before you know it, your pup will bring his ball to you each time you roll it. Remember to call the dog each time he returns to you and be sure to use the same word.

Being a baby he may occasionally tease you by running away with the ball. If he does this frequently, put a short rope on his collar and gently pull him toward you as soon as he has the ball in his mouth. Call him by name and urge him to come. Praise him repeatedly, even if you have pulled him to you.

Since your puppy is young and has a very short attention span, it's best to limit your lessons to about five minutes, two or three times a day.

Remember, make sure your puppy wants to come to you. Use a pleasant, happy voice when calling him. Occasionally give your pup a tidbit to eat as a reward for coming when you called. *Never call your dog to come to you if he needs discipline. If you call him and then hit him, he will not be so anxious to come to you again. All his life he must associate coming to you with love and praise.*

BUILDING VOCABULARY

By now you realize that you have already taught your dog three things. You have taught him four words: "come, fetch, ball and give." You've also taught him the beginning rules in the game of "come." Most important of all, you are teaching him that you are "top dog" in your home, by setting a few rules which he must follow.

If you started the game of "fetch the ball" very early in the pup's life, your puppy should be bringing the ball to you very well by the time he is four or five months old. It's fun to watch a young pup play this game. He's firmly convinced there is no smarter dog in the world, and dances in anticipation while waiting for you to roll or throw the ball.

Now is the time to teach your dog that he must "come when called" with or without the ball. This can also be done easily and playfully. All learning should be fun for the young pup, and his continuing eagerness to learn is a credit to you as his teacher.

TEACHING PUPPY "COME" OUT OF DOORS

Here is a simple fun lesson to continue teaching "come when called."

Place a six to eight-foot rope on the pup's collar and

take him for a walk. Let him wander to the end of the rope, sniffing the ground and enjoying himself. When you see his attention is on something other than you, call him. He probably won't pay any attention to you and that's just what you want.

Call him again and gently pull him to you with the leash, being sure to praise him as he comes. You may even give him an occasional tidbit when he obeys. Be insistent that he come to you, even if you have to pull him. When he comes be sure to praise him with a happy "you're the best dog in the world" voice.

After your pup has returned to you a number of times while on the short leash, start using a longer rope. Twenty feet of lightweight rope or twine is just about the right length. Follow the same rules with the longer rope and by the time your dog is six months old, you will have a happy dog running to you eagerly.

This eagerness can be overdone though, as I learned when I trained my first dog. We were living in Detroit at the time that I enrolled my boxer named Heidi in an obedience class. We both worked hard in school and I was very proud of her.

On graduation night we were required to go through an obedience trial to receive our diplomas. Everything went well for Heidi and me until the "recall" or "call your dog." I gave Heidi a good firm "sit, stay" command, turned and walked about 25 feet away, then stood facing her. On command from the judge I told Heidi to "come."

From her first leap I knew what was coming. The audience gasped as I stood frozen, waiting for the inevitable. Heidi came with all of the enthusiasm that only a boxer can have. Well, she knocked me flat amid the laughter of my classmates and judge.

You'll have to admit, she did come when called. However after that incident I put the "darn fool dog" back on her leash and taught her how to "sit" when she came to me.

"COME" "SIT" "STAY"

By the time your puppy is five or six months old he should eagerly come to you every time you call him. Let's keep him happy by teaching him more learning tricks you both will enjoy.

When you taught your dog to "come when called," you also taught him four words: "come, fetch, give, and ball." Now it's time to increase his vocabulary by adding three new words: "sit, stay," and "release."

Until now as your dog returned to you, he has jumped on you, licked your face, and in general acted just like any young pup would. To prevent him from becoming a compulsive jumper and teach him more self-control, he will now return to you with his ball, sit in front of you, wait for you to take the ball, then release him. Try this simple method and you'll be amazed with the results.

When your dog is running happily toward you with the ball in his mouth, bend forward and firmly put him in the "sit" position, with his nose and toes facing you, six inches away from your knees. As you push his tail to the floor say "sit and stay." Praise him while you make him sit and do not hold him down for long. A young pup is just too excited to sit still for long periods of time. Next, tell him to "give" and take the ball from his mouth. Now say "release" or "OK" to tell him the lesson is over and he may play if he wishes. For the thousandth time tell him how wonderful he is.

Practice this lesson for a few weeks and soon your puppy will run to you and sit holding his ball. He will then "sit and stay" until you take the ball, "release" and praise him.

Of course, this lesson of "sit and stay" should be carried into everyday living. Every time your dog comes to you he should "sit" and "wait" for your attention. It is important that you give him as much praise when he "sits" as he would get by jumping on you.

When a guest enters your house tell your pup to "sit and stay" and ask your guest to pet him and praise his good behavior. Remember, no one likes to be jumped on or slobbered all over by your dog. In fact, none of your friends can enjoy a dog with poor behavior. If your dog lacks self-discipline it's not his fault, it's yours. Your dog is a creature of habit and you set the habits, not him.

When your dog "comes when called" and "sits" until "released," you will have a happy pup that you'll enjoy living with. If he learns these lessons at an early age, he will excel in obedience class.

DOG COLLARS—FASHIONABLE AND PRACTICAL

Since dog first licked man's hand instead of biting it, collars of every shape, texture, and color have been placed on his neck. Through the ages collars have been used for adornment, control and safety.

The Egyptians, as early as 2,700 B.C., made collars of precious metals in the shape of laurel leaves overlapping each other.

Tablets and inscriptions from 5,000 to 6,000 B.C. picture dogs with collars of wide leather, embroidered and encrusted with jewels.

James I, King of England, hunted boar and wolf with mastiff dogs who wore wide iron collars with spikes "the length of a man's middle finger." Meanwhile, the queen

and her ladies were weaving garlands of flowers to adorn their "wee lappe dogges."

Fancy collars of velvet and satin, embroidered and jeweled still adorn many dogs today. These collars are fine for special occasions but every dog must have a strong comfortable collar that holds its license, rabies and identification tags. For their own protection, dogs should never be without their tags.

There are three basic materials used for both collars and leashes: nylon, leather and chain.

Leather is attractive, durable and functional, but also deceiving because quality is so varied. Check the following to assure that you are buying leather. The product should be marked genuine leather. It should smell like leather, and also be priced higher than imitation leather. Genuine leather will last longer, resist water and feel comfortable on your dog's neck as well as in your hand. Leather is also the most expensive to buy, but even the widest leash is reasonably priced and will last throughout a dog's life, if cared for properly.

Nylon is strong, durable and washable. It also is comfortable for both you and your dog. The biggest problem with nylon is that it slips through your hand. This is a real nuisance if you are trying to control an active dog. If you can find a nylon leash that doesn't slip it will work fine. I have not found any nylon leash that compares with good leather.

Any chain product is only as good as its weakest link. Before purchasing a chain collar or leash be sure you check each link for weakness. A chain link collar is inexpensive and an absolute must for training your dog. Using a chain collar is also the most humane method for training and discipline.

Even though chain leashes are cheap they bruise the hands if used with an active dog. Chain leashes are never used in obedience work because they rattle against the metal training collar and confuse the dog.

Here are a few final tips concerning collars:

DO NOT LEAVE YOUR dog alone, tied by his training collar. Many dogs have died choked by their chain collars.

BE SURE THAT the leather collar or leash you purchase has the clasp or ring sewn on rather than riveted. Sewing is much stronger and rivets tend to pop.

TO PREVENT YOUR dog from mouthing or chewing on his leash put a few dabs of Tabasco sauce on the material.

If we think we are ridiculous about our dogs today, think about the past. During the eighteenth century in Victorian England the idle rich paid the best literary men in the country to write poetry suitable for dog collars. For a lap dog named Tiger, Jonathan Swift composed:

"Pray steal me not, I'm Mrs Dingliy's
Whose heart in this four-footed thing lies."

WALKING TOGETHER

Since walking quietly is difficult for a young dog, I prefer to start "heeling" lessons at five or six months. By this time, canine muscles and brain are developing well and the dog has greater control over his body and emotions.

Your pup is now older and has learned the few rules necessary for a happy life with his family. The time has come for him to wear his training collar and learn to walk beside you like a little gentleman or lady, and sit when you stop. You will be amply rewarded for your efforts when friends and neighbors compliment you on your well-behaved dog.

When heeling properly, your dog must keep pace with you, neither suddenly lunging ahead nor lagging behind. His shoulder should be as close to your left knee as possible without touching. The dog stays in this position whether you walk, run, turn about, or go in circles. When you stop, the pup should sit squarely next to your left foot and remain in this position until you give another command.

HEELING ON LEASH

Obedience classes teach that when leaving the dog, give a firm vocal "stay" command and walk forward, right foot first. You may then walk forward to the end of the lead, turn confidently and face him. Remain quiet for a few minutes to be sure your pet will obey the command.

Then walk around the dog to the heeling position once again. To release your dog, say "OK" or "release", and give him a playful hug to reassure him that there just isn't any dog as smart as your dog.

When the dog is to go with you, the left foot will be the first foot out. This is an excellent silent signal to let your pet know whether he must stay or go along. You will be amazed how rapidly dogs pick up this body language. I'm sure all of my dogs spot the foot movement before I have given the voice command.

As you step forward briskly on the left foot, using a firm voice, say, "Rover, heel." At the same time, give your leash a snap to bring the dog immediately into motion. Of course you will use your dog's name and snap the leash according to his age and size. Don't forget to praise that good dog as he starts to heel.

To help your dog understand the stop and go movements in heeling, shorten the leash in your left hand as you glide into a halt. Using your right hand, pull upward and backward on the leash as you tap or push the dog on the rump into a sitting position. Done quickly and firmly, the dog is sitting before he has a chance to object. Leave him as is for a few minutes. Now release him with an "OK" as you pat your leg to invite play. Once again tell him how wonderful he is.

As we work together, I usually talk, click my tongue, tell jokes, and chatter on about how wonderful, intelligent, and obedient my best friend is. Making a game out of learning is just as important for dogs as it is for children. I have never entered a dog in an obedience show when the dog has not acted as though this was the most fun ever.

Your dog loves to communicate with you. If you won't lick him in return, at least talk and play with him.

NO JUMPING

One day last week, to make a rainy, miserable day even worse, I realized it was my turn to drive the school car pool.

As I pushed the gang of children out the back door to run for the car, a lonely, half grown, part English Setter ran up and jumped on my coat leaving mud streaks.

Of course he was only a baby, so I resisted the urge to strangle the little darling and instead put him into the garage. A short time later he was happily reunited with his family.

While I scrubbed the mud off my coat I started thinking about what an ordeal most of us go through teaching our dogs not to leap on us.

The reason for this troublesome habit probably is our own inconsistency.

When our dogs bark, bite, or dig up the yard, we are annoyed and correct the dog immediately.

When our dog affectionately jumps on us while we are wearing old clothes however, our hard hearts melt and we respond with affection.

Let him jump on our good suit or ruin our best nylons though, and we give him a swat and tell him "no."

What does this do to our dog? It leaves him confused.

There is a simple solution for this confused dog and his sometimes compassionate, sometimes angry owner: Teach the pet not to jump on anyone except by invitation.

Teaching your dog not to jump on you is simple. In fact if the pup is small, all you have to do is put his feet firmly back on the floor and say "no" when he jumps. You must do this each time he jumps and really mean "no" when you say it.

When correcting an older or larger dog, bring up your knee and push against the dog's chest as he jumps, of course, saying "no" again. Once again, catching him and making the correction each time he jumps is very important.

Because your dog already knows what "no" means, he will connect the knee push and the voice command very quickly. Within a short time your dog will resist his impulse to jump and keep all four feet on the floor where they belong.

JUMPING BY INVITATION

When your dog has learned his lesson well and no longer jumps, you may then teach him to jump up. But only when you give him permission.

Again this is ridiculously simple. Bend forward and pat your knees, inviting your dog to put his paws upon you. At the same time say "OK, OK." *Be sure your voice is cheerful and inviting.*

The first few times puppy will resist the invitation as he knows this is forbidden. Reassure him by picking up his front feet and placing them on your knees, or shoulders if tall, again saying "OK, good dog." He'll soon understand your invitation and be absolutely delighted.

Now you and your dog are both happy and you both know the exact rules of the game. It's the best of both worlds when you can have an obedient companion, as well as a happy, fun-loving friend.

TALK TO ANIMALS WITH KEY WORDS

Any dog with normal intelligence is capable of understanding a large vocabulary. As I have said before, dogs learn by repetition. Certainly a dog who is with people most of the time has the advantage of learning more than an animal isolated in the back yard.

I constantly am amazed at some of the vocabulary our dogs understand, although our family has made no effort to teach these words.

The word "egg" is an example. Say "egg" to our Sheltie, Kilty, and she goes into spasms of joy. An egg is the equivalent of a "hot fudge sundae" to the canines in our house. I'm sure over the years, I have said "egg" each time I've offered one to Kilty, but I don't remember saying it. Since she enjoys them so much, she remembers and associates the word with good food.

Most people who enjoy the companionship of their dogs talk to them like friends. Our dogs not only enjoy hearing our voices during these moments, but also learn and associate key words.

By key words I mean that we may say a long sentence and our dogs may respond to the sounds. But actually they are listening and understanding only one or two key words. The key word is the only important word in our dogs' understanding.

For instance say, "It's time to go outside and play ball in the yard." The dog probably will understand only two words. The word "out" is familiar since we have used it while training the dog to go outside. "Ball" means play, and our dog eagerly remembers this word and associates it with running.

Even though we use complete sentences when talking to our dog, we need only key words. In the above sentence, all we needed to say was "out" and "ball."

As humans with large vocabularies, we enjoy using complete sentences even though they are not important to our dogs. Therefore it is important to remember to use short sentences when talking to your dog and equally important to emphasize the key words.

Our dogs enjoy words requiring an action response. We can say "please" and "thank you" to our dog but he cannot understand the words unless we accompany it with an action. I have found that occasionally I say "thank you" instead of "good dog" when praising my dogs. I also pat them on the head at the same time. Recently I noticed that it makes no difference whether I say "good dog" or "thank you." The dogs associate both with praise.

I never have found any action for the word "please," even though I often hear people in my class use it. However "please" does have a pleasant sound even if the dog does not understand the meaning.

Here are some key words that your dog can associate with an action. Almost any dog, at any age, can learn and will enjoy the action once taught the key word.

KEY WORDS	ACTION
Sit up	Lift front paws off floor while sitting
Shake or "gimme" five	Place paw in owner's hand
Outside	Go out the door
Bye bye or car	Get into car for ride
No	Stop what you are doing
Quiet	Stop barking or making noise
Down	Lie down
Rug or bed	Go to your rug or bed
Stay	Remain where you are
Cookie, egg, candy	Food

TEACHING YOUR DOG TO RIDE IN AUTO

Dog behavior is shaped as much by environment as by bloodline. Just as parents raise a well-adjusted child by exposing him to new places, new faces and good education, the family dog should also be exposed to positive experiences.

Allowing a child to grow up in a home without love and companionship will help make a hostile, unhappy adult.

The same is true of a dog who is not exposed to the outside world while still a pup. The earlier a puppy is acquainted with other dogs and people, the sooner it will understand that it lives in a loving, fun-filled environment.

Occasionally our family enjoys taking our dogs along on vacation. It can be enjoyable if owners have taken the time and energy to prepare the dogs for the long hours of riding in a car.

44

Many dogs, if not prepared in advance, get car sick even on short trips. Long rides with a nervous canine can ruin the entire family's fun. Whether taking your dog on a vacation or just to the local market, start now with these few training suggestions and your happy pet will not only eagerly jump into the car as soon as you rattle the keys, but be a pleasant companion as well.

When taking your dog into the car for the first time, place the dog where you wish him to stay whenever he is in the car. If your dog is a quivering mess, sit in the correct spot and place the dog in your lap. Leave the nearest car door open and the motor off. Pat, reassure and soothe your friend for a few minutes. Then remove him from the car and praise him for being so brave.

Repeat this procedure frequently for a few days and gradually lengthen the time in the car. A few tasty tidbits to eat may also be given to the dog in the car at any time during the training.

Within a few days the dog should be happy to jump into the car and sit where you trained him to stay. I like to teach the dog to sit on a rug on the back seat. It's just as easy to teach him to sit on a rug, and frequently this prevents the car seat from being soiled by muddy or wet paws.

When the dog is content to sit in the car, start the engine. If you think that the noise will make the dog nervous, have someone else start the engine while you sit by the dog giving reassurance.

Now is a good time for a distraction! How about a dog

biscuit or a few raisins to take your pet's attention away from the engine noise.

Repeat all training. Gradually add the buzz of the seat belt until the pet has no qualms about entering the car and ignores all noises.

Once the dog enjoys the car and ignores the noises, you can drive up and down the driveway or around the block. Be sure to make the first trips short and pleasant.

LIBRA AND THE CAR

My doggone son of a poodle Libra is the car-lovingest dog I've ever seen.

Just mention the words "bye bye" while grabbing the car keys and this giant will flatten anyone trying to get out the door ahead of her.

I overcame this problem within a short time by making Libra "sit and stay" before opening the door.

I now can leave the house with dignity and clothes intact, hold open the door after exiting and say "OK." The mad dash for the car made by the dog doesn't bother me at all, because I can take my time, get out of the dog's path and walk to the car without tripping over her.

Once we are both outside and about to enter the car, I repeat the procedure.

I have a rug at one side of the back seat that Libra must sit on.

Previously when I opened the door, she dashed into the car and often would collide with the assorted packages, toys or clothing left on the rear seat by the family. By teaching her good manners and insisting that she sit outside and wait until told to enter the car, I have time to open the door, remove anything necessary and straighten Libra's rug.

When I again say "OK" Libra jumps into the car, sits on the rug and happily watches all of the action on the sidewalk during her ride.

Don't think I am altogether heartless. I admit to parking as close as possible to the doors of the stores because I know how much Libra enjoys seeing people. I take her on these trips as much as possible, although at times I leave the store sooner than planned since she is waiting in the car.

INSIST YOUR DOG USES GOOD MANNERS

It surprises me that many people ask for help with a training problem when they already have the solution, as I did, but don't use it.

Once you have taught your dog to sit and stay, you must remember to use the command at the right time. When a visitor enters your home, and your dog is a "jump up and lick the face" kind of lover, you must control the situation by telling the dog to "sit and stay." Ask your guest to pet the dog to reassure him that he will always get the attention he wants by behaving correctly.

When you say "no" you are telling your dog to stop whatever he is doing, stay where he is, and wait for your command. If your dog started to cross the street, you would naturally say "no" and then "stay" to emphasize the command. Once he has obeyed your command, you may then retrieve and praise him, or call him and praise him when he comes.

If you have taught your dog to go to his bed, rug or corner, you should give the command to go, then immediately follow that command with the word "stay." Your dog then knows that he must go to his spot and remain in that spot until released, or given another command such as "come."

Why not take a few days and watch how your family uses the obedience training you have given your dog. Are you using it effectively, or have you allowed your dog to become demanding and impatient? If you don't like your pet's behavior, it's time to have a family discussion, correct the bad behavior and start enjoying your dog again.

KEEP YOUR DOG COOL

Walk through any parking lot on a hot summer day and count the dogs in cars waiting patiently for their owners.

Walk down any street in the city or suburbs and listen to the dogs barking behind closed garage doors. These dog owners needlessly risk the lives of their dogs from heat stroke, a summer killer.

Dogs and cats do not perspire. The only cooling system they have for an over-heated body is panting. When a dog is exposed to temperatures that build up in enclosed areas, such as a car, his panting may become excessive. In extreme cases, the panting may become so strenuous that it makes him hotter instead of cooler.

Soon the blood vessels begin to dilate and lack of increased blood circulation causes the vessels to collapse. The dog then goes into severe shock, brain damage results, and death follows.

Heat exhaustion and sun stroke can be prevented with a little common sense and caution.

DO NOT TAKE your dog in the car for shopping trips in extremely hot weather. You may be in the store longer than you think and a car can quickly become an oven even with the windows open. Fido would be much happier at home keeping his cool by the air conditioner.

ALWAYS PROVIDE A cool area for your dog to stay during the hottest part of the day.

DON'T CONFINE YOUR dog in close quarters where the heat can build up and the air can stagnate.

DON'T ALLOW YOUR dog to become overweight. Fat dogs have heat strokes faster than thin dogs.

DON'T LET YOUR dog exercise vigorously during the hottest part of the day. Early morning and evening are cooler and safer.

GIVE YOUR DOG plenty of fresh, cool water. In fact, most dogs enjoy chewing on an ice cube when it is hot outside.

DON'T ASSUME THAT your dog knows when to stop playing and get out of the sun. Our family dog almost had a heat stroke last summer while playing with the children in the hot sun. Fortunately, the children noticed the dog's heavy panting and we hosed her down with tap water to cool her.

The normal temperature of a dog is between 100 and 102 degrees. If your dog's temperature rises to 104 or 105 degrees, he is in trouble.

If you think your dog is developing heat stroke, immediately cool him with water. When traveling, even a stream or ditch filled with water will do. Then keep your pet quiet so his body heat will decrease. If he doesn't revive immediately find a veterinarian fast. You don't have much time with heat stroke.

An ounce of prevention is worthwhile for both you and your dog. Follow these suggestions and your dog will have a happy, healthy summer.

PRACTICE, PATIENCE AND PRAISE

Every dog has a natural desire to please his master. In fact, dog is the only animal on earth who willingly obeys with no reward but a word of praise. To help you give that praise more often, here are a few final hints.

KEEP YOUR PUPPY confined when you cannot watch him. If you do not have a pen, use a short rope on a collar to tie him near his bed, food and water.

FEED YOUR PUP a nutritious dry kibble that is recommended for puppies. Add vitamins and high-protein table scraps such as cottage cheese, meat, and cooked egg when you can. Moisten with a little water or milk. Be careful about starting your puppy on expensive canned or dehydrated meat. Your 10-pound pup may become a 60 to 70-pound adult dog.

PLACE YOUR PUP'S dish in the same spot each feeding and leave his food for only 10 to 20 minutes. Remove the dish and do not feed him again until the next scheduled feeding. This will keep up his appetite and prevent him from becoming a fussy eater.

ONCE OR TWICE a week remove the dog's food while he is eating. After a few seconds put the food back and tell him he is a good dog. If he growls, correct him promptly. Do not allow your dog to be possessive about his food. If you continue this procedure until he is an adult, he will never growl or bite, even if a stranger takes something from his mouth.

PROVIDE HIM WITH a warm bed away from household noise and confusion. Like any baby, he needs lots of sleep. Be sure he gets his rest when he wants or needs it.

TEACH YOUR PUPPY to be alone. All of his life there will be occasions when you will have to leave him in the house alone. Provide him with chew toys, water and his bed. Now, make sure you resist his crying for attention.

He will soon learn to relax and wait patiently for your return.

SINCE EVERYONE LOVES to hold a puppy, teach the children to sit on the floor to hold the dog and you'll never have a puppy injured by jumping from their arms.

BE FIRM BUT don't overdo the discipline. Your pup is still a baby with a short memory. If you're really having a bad day, isolate the pup. Don't take your bad temper out on him.

AN EXCELLENT WAY to discipline your dog is to use a rolled newspaper, but not on the dog. Smack your hand with the paper, and at the same time say "no." The noise from the newspaper together with your voice will startle and distract him. After the correction, remove him from the scene of the crime.

PLAN TO HAVE your dog neutered while he or she is young. In times of high prices, it is difficult to place your litters and animal shelters become overcrowded. It's much more humane to prevent puppies than to have them killed.

YOUR DOG MUST always think he is a success. Be sure to praise good behavior.

MAKE RAISING YOUR puppy a family experience. Even the youngest child will enjoy the responsibility of feeding and caring for his or her best friend.

A list of the puppy's schedule taped to the refrigerator door is an excellent way for the whole family to remember what to do and when to do it. A second list taped beside the schedule should inform the family of the activities the pup may or may not do. If everything is written down, no one can use that old excuse of forgetting.

Now relax. Keep your sense of humor and enjoy your dog. With a little common sense, foresight and knowledge, raising your pup isn't half as bad as you thought. In fact, it will be downright enjoyable.

Part 2

Nobody's Home Dog
Grows Up

DOG'S PURPOSE ON EARTH

One day God and St. Peter were strolling along the pathways of heaven when a dog passed beside them.

God patted the dog and spoke kindly to the animal. "What is that?" asked St. Peter.

"It's a dog," replied God. "Do you want to know why I made him?"

"Yes," said Peter. "Tell me about the dog."

"Well you know how much trouble the devil has made for me," said God. "He made me drive Adam and Eve out of Paradise. The poor people nearly starved.

"They didn't know how to find food. The poor things nearly froze. They didn't know how to find clothes. So I gave my people sheep for meat and wool to keep them warm. Then, that nasty fellow Lucifer made a giant reptile to harass my people and destroy the sheep.

"So I made a dog. I made it white as a symbol of purity, fidelity and love. I gave this animal four feet for swiftness. I gave it large ears that it could hear all sounds. I gave it a voice like thunder, that it might frighten evil. Last of all, I gave dog large teeth that it might battle for good over evil.

"My people are now safe," concluded God. "Dog will guard the flocks. He will keep man and his possessions safe for all generations to come."

Rumanian Folklore

COMMUNICATION—KEY TO SUCCESSFUL TRAINING

When training a dog, the trainer's inner feelings are just as important as the physical actions used. Proper equipment, voice control and physical movements are necessary, but aren't enough. Having the correct attitude or inner feeling toward the dog is an absolute must for successful training.

Feelings mandated from the owner to the dog carry this most important message: "I respect you enough to know that you will not be happy if you do not understand the rules you must live by. Therefore, you must learn to obey my commands."

All of this is transmitted immediately to the dog—not only by handling, but by an inner communication existing between man and dog.

A professional dog trainer will take a strange dog firmly by the leash, give it a command, and the dog will obey.

An amateur using the same words and handling the dog the same way may have poor results. The difference? The professional dog trainer has an inner assurance that this dog, any dog, has the right to be taught to live within the rules of human society.

What the amateur trainer fails to understand is that the professional has a deep affection and respect for all canines. Even more, the professional understands the frustration and loneliness a dog suffers from lack of proper training. Few humans can tolerate living with an untrained or poorly trained dog.

A command given to your dog with good inner attitude and proper procedure can be said in a whisper and the dog, feeling the trainer's confidence in it, will obey.

Owners must feel this communication and use it at all times when giving their dogs a command. This is the secret to successful dog training and anyone can do it. *Remember that love does not mean permissiveness and obedience does not mean cruelty.*

We all know people who think obedience training should be done with a heavy hand. The rest of us believe that a combination of kindness, firmness and common sense, mixed with lots of love will be more effective.

Now that your pup is half grown, you should have a moderately well-behaved companion. The dog still requires continued training, but it should be comfortably toilet trained and well-behaved if you have been alert and prevented bad habits.

"DOWN" "STAY"

Your dog is familiar with the words "come, sit, stay." Now is the time to teach your dog to lie down on command. Teaching your dog to "sit, stay" before the "down" makes this lesson easier.

Unless your dog is a toy breed, you should purchase a chain link training collar for discipline and control. Place the collar on the dog's neck with the surplus chain going over the ring and toward the top of the neck. Once the dog is used to the collar, most of your discipline should be accompanied by a sharp corrective jerk. At the same time be sure there is firmness and determination in your voice.

To teach your dog to lie down, place him in the "sit, stay" position. Squat, facing your dog's left side. Tell him "down" and at the same time lift his paws upward and forward with the left hand and push the dog's shoulders toward the floor with your right hand. Hold the dog down, say "stay" which he already knows and praise his great intelligence. A few minutes later, release him with an "OK" or "release" command.

Between lessons play with your pup. This will make the

lesson fun and less tiresome for both of you. Repeat the "down" lesson three or four times each evening. Make sure the dog goes down and remains until released. You may have to hold him "down" for the first few lessons.

Once the dog is toilet trained and learns to lie down on command, he will quickly adjust to sleeping in another area. Tie the dog to the bedstead or table nearby and insist that he remain in that place quietly until released in the morning. This is one good way to prevent the young dog from forming the habit of soiling other areas of the house during your sleeping hours. The first few nights you may have to reassure your pet a few times, but soon he will eagerly run to his rug, pillow or bed each evening.

Try to relax, keep your lessons short and although you must be insistent and firm, have fun while your puppy is learning. Never make the "sit" or "down" lesson too long while the pup is young. Gradually lengthen the lesson as the pup matures. This is a good time to give your young dog the privilege of sleeping in an area other than the small pen. Our dogs enjoy sleeping beside our beds at night, and I can find no reason not to allow it, as long as they behave.

OBEDIENCE CLASS

From four to six months of age a puppy learns quickly and usually loves attending a kinder-pup obedience class when one is available. If not, try to put your pup in a beginning obedience class at around six months. With the home training you have given your dog, I guarantee you will be overjoyed at the difference in the behavior of your well-trained dog when you compare him with the wild acting canines enrolled in your class.

There are good and bad obedience instructors. The good teachers will be interested in each dog in their classes. They will give you information about training your special breed. They will know that Schnauzers hate to heel, and Dobermans lie like a spring, ready to leap. They will speak to you with courtesy and understanding. When handling your dog they will be firm with no nonsense. They will not coddle you or your dog. They will insist that you both learn. You will love the classes and be happy you spent the time and money.

The bad teachers are rude to their classes, yell at the people and can ruin your dog by abuse. *The only time a dog must be treated severely is for biting.* Even then they should not be beaten. Snapping dogs should have their mouths grabbed and closed; they should be shaken and spoken to loudly with authority. You must wear gloves if you are an amateur at this. For heaven's sake, if your dog might bite—warn your obedience instructor. He or she can't help you or your dog if they are not aware of the problem. Furthermore, an innocent bystander might get hurt.

If you find yourself enrolled in a poor class, don't quit. Let the instructor know that you absolutely will not allow your dog to be hit. Stand your ground and try to learn.

There will be times during your dog training class when the collar jerking may look too severe. Have confidence in your teacher and give him or her a few weeks to work out the problems. Usually by the third week the dogs calm down. The class work from then on becomes orderly, interesting and fun.

CARRIE AND KILTY

For many years our family talked about putting a swimming pool in the back yard. Finally, after measuring our small city lot and pinching pennies, our dream came true. We signed a contract and the work began.

Day after day, our little pre-schooler Carrie sat with our elderly neighbor on his back porch. Carrie's little Sheltie, Kilty, always beside them, helped supervise the construction.

As the weeks went past, the three friends grew weary, but rarely strayed from their porch with the superior view.

It was an exciting time in the life of our four-year-old. Along with discussions about the pool the family also was concerned because Kilty was in heat and had to be carefully watched.

The busy days passed and the time finally came when water flowed by the hour to fill the large hole in the ground.

As Carrie chatted merrily, her old friend interjected a sudden thought. "Bet you'll be the first one to jump into the pool, eh Carrie?" he said.

"Oh no," replied our daughter, suddenly serious, "Kilty's in heat and I've been waiting to throw her in the pool to cool her off."

Carrie no longer remembers Kilty's first heat. We had the veterinarian spay the dog a few months later.

Did Kilty get grouchy or lose her sweet disposition? Did she get fat while still young? Did she become lazy and lose her pep and energy? Did denying her a sex life bother her in any way?

The answer to all of these questions is "no." And if the answer is "no" for our dog, it will be the same for yours.

Kilty did not get fat because we did not allow her to overeat before she was spayed and we do not allow her to overeat now. Your dog, like ours, can gain weight only by overeating. Kilty did not become lazy after surgery because she had plenty of room to exercise, toys to play with, and a loving family to stimulate activity. Do you do the same for your dog?

After she was spayed, did Kilty mourn her missing sex life? The answer is "no." By having her spayed, we didn't really deny Kilty a sex life. *Animal sex is biological stimulation and is not retained in the memory.*

In other words, Kilty is happy, unrestrained and has a long life expectancy.

Had either of our dogs been a male, he would have been castrated when he was six to nine months old.

Neutering does not make either male or female dogs less protective of their home and family. On the other hand castrated males definitely are less inclined to fight other dogs over territorial rights. Many owners of adult male dogs that have not been castrated have been forced to pay costly vet bills because their dogs attacked and injured other dogs.

Castration of the male dog will not make him fat, lazy or inactive. He, like a neutered female, will become less inclined to roam, cleaner to live with and won't miss a sex life he neither experienced nor remembered.

There is nothing wrong with calling several vets in your area to find out the estimated cost of neutering. Usually a male operation will cost less than one for the female and require a shorter stay in the hospital.

Since there is a significant price difference in surgical costs, you will usually be told that "it all depends on the

65

size of your dog.'' When this happens, be ready to tell the dog's height, weight, sex and approximate breed if it is a mutt. Find out if your surgical cost will include medicine, stitch removal (usually free), and all other expenses. Be sure to ask how many days the dog will be hospitalized.

Many conscientious veterinarians prefer to keep a dog for three days after surgery. Other vets release their cats and dogs within twenty-four hours. A three-day visit, of course, raises the cost of the operation.

If you have a physically healthy animal with no medical problems, request the price of twenty-four-hour hospitalization.

Few veterinary hospitals have staff in the building during the night hours. I prefer to bring my pets home where I can keep an eye on them all night.

When you must drive a long distance for an emergency, or the dog must stay alone all day, you may prefer to leave your pet with the vet for the full three-day period.

PUPPY WETTING

Many of the letters and phone calls I receive concern problems with puppies under one year old. Most of these problems can be solved with consistent discipline and training. When you have an unusual problem, there are times when the solution you find doesn't seem at all related to your situation.

My latest call for help concerned a nine-month-old pup with weak bladder muscles. Every time the pup got excited, her bladder dripped. This is a common problem and it does not relate to toilet training. Some dogs have bladder problems and some don't. There is no way of choosing beforehand which pup will or won't have this difficulty. My poodle, Libra, has had this problem to a small extent for two years. Most often, as the bladder muscles mature, these dogs will stop the involuntary wetting, usually by the time they are about one year old.

With Libra, the problem has not been eliminated entirely, but I do have the situation under control. The answer I found most effective for Libra and all other dogs is: *teach the dog to "sit" on command.*

Involuntary wetting usually occurs at moments of excitement or stress. For example, the owner returns after leaving the dog alone, or a stranger approaches the dog. When frightened or disciplined, this apprehensive dog squats as a hand is extended toward him. In the squatting position, the bladder muscles relax and the poor dog wets. The dog is unaware of this action and therefore is unable to solve the problem. You, the owner, knowing what is about to happen, should immediately upon seeing the dog squat, lean forward over your pet and push the dog's bottom firmly to the floor. *A dog cannot wet while sitting.* With determination in your voice and action, tell your dog to "sit, stay," then happily praise his obedience.

It is important that you keep the dog sitting until he is calm. When the dog is quiet, say "OK" or "release" and once again praise the wonderful behavior.

Making your dog "sit and stay" in this situation takes firm self-discipline for the dog, and a strong desire on your part to solve the problem. It is well worth the time and effort. You will be happier with an obedient dog who wets only on rare occasions rather than daily. Your dog will bask in the love and affection he receives for his good behavior.

INNER DETERMINATION

When we give our dogs a voice command, but our inner feeling does not support that command, our pets become confused and unhappy.

We must transmit the message, "You must do as I say," while we are saying it. Our dogs will then understand unmistakably what to do and make every effort to obey. Our reward will be a well-trained happy dog which can be praised instead of punished for its behavior.

Recently while watching a class of owners heel their dogs around the ring during the third week, I was appalled to see dragging, tugging and yelling taking place.

Some classes are great, some are average, but this was terrible.

Once again I explained the proper use of collar and leash to the handlers. Most of all, I wanted to impress on them the importance of using the "positive attitude" when working with their dogs. This inner determination is quickly transmitted to the dog by the handler's body language, and voice. I suggested that anyone using both the correct mental and physical procedures would have the dog under control in a short time.

Choosing a frolicking, happy-go-lucky, half-grown husky, I demonstrated that anyone, using a firm "no nonsense" attitude along with the proper use of leash and collar, will have an obedient dog within a short time.

The pup I was working stopped jumping after the first time around the ring. The second circuit, he heeled correctly and even sat on command as we halted.

The class seemed to be impressed. Most of all, I felt the trainers understood that if I could make a strange dog behave, they could control their own pets.

During intermission most class members took their dogs for a walk out of doors. As one young couple passed, I noticed that the collar on their young German Shepherd had been put on incorrectly. Being emphatically assured by the young man that his dog would not bite me, I bent close to change the collar. As my face came near the dog's mouth, he gave a sharp snap and I quickly pulled away. I came so close to being bitten that I could feel the moisture from the dog's mouth on my cheek.

Shocked and surprised, I angrily said, "I thought you said that your dog wouldn't bite." Confused and painfully embarrassed, the young man stammered, "Why ma'am, he has given me a nip or two, but I never dreamed he'd have the nerve to bite YOU!"

It was humorous and I laughed about it at the time, especially since I hadn't been bitten. Later I felt sad when realizing that the young man had not understood the real meaning of my class demonstration.

I was saying, "Everyone can train his dog if he communicates with it," and the young man was thinking, "Only the teacher can do it!"

If we humans have a hard time communicating while speaking the same language, how confused our dogs must become when we either fail to transmit our message to them or send them a mixed-up command.

HOW TO MAKE A NYLON PULL TOY

It's a common sight in our house to see any member of the family sitting in a comfortable chair reading, with a book in one hand and our dog's nylon pull toy in the other.

The dog growls ferociously, shakes her head and pulls with all of her strength.

Tug-o-war has been a favorite game with all of our dogs. We make our pull toys out of old nylon stockings. I guarantee both you and your dog will enjoy using this fun toy which is extremely easy to make.

If you have a medium-sized dog (15 to 22 inches), you will need nine single stockings. For a smaller dog use six. A German Shepherd, Husky, or St. Bernard will need 12.

If you work in multiples of three, you can make any size necessary for your dog. Panty hose or opaque hose work too. Don't cut the tops off until you finish the toy even if you use panty hose.

Run all of the stockings through the washer and dryer, and then you are ready to start.

Tie all of the stockings together with one knot at the top. Place the knot above the sheer part and well into the reinforced material. *Make the knot very tight. This is the secret.*

After you have the knot made, put three medium-sized children or one adult at each end and pull hard to tighten. It sounds bulky to work with, but nylon slides easily and is enjoyable to handle.

When you have the tightest knot possible, you're ready to start braiding. Don't let your helpers get away. You'll need them until you're finished.

Divide the nine stockings into three sections of three stockings each. With twelve stockings divide into three sections of four each.

With your helper holding the knot to keep the work taut, start braiding the sections. This braiding must also be very tight. After each section of braiding, push the braid toward the knot as firmly as possible.

Make a smooth, tight braid almost the length of the stocking. You will have to leave enough material to put another strong knot at the other end of the braid.

The braid when finished will be about 15 to 17 inches long. If yours is much longer than 17 inches, undo the braid and make a tighter one.

Remember, your dog will be pulling and stretching this toy as he plays with it.

When the braid is finished, tie another knot very tightly and push the knot toward the braid. You should leave two or three inches of material above each knot to cut off and make a fringe.

You and your dog now have a neat, attractive pull toy that is safe, clean and fun to play with.

With knots at each end, you and your dog can get a firm grip for your tug-o-war. The nylon is soft and easy on both your hands and the dog's mouth.

Double the braid in your hand and throw it like a ball. It's just as much fun for your dog to retrieve and it won't break your table top decorations if it accidentally hits them.

With continued play, your dog will pull some pieces of nylon out of the braid. If some of the nylon is accidentally swallowed by the dog, it will pass safely through the stomach without puncturing vital parts. However to be extra safe, trim off any snags with the scissors until the toy gets too ragged to use.

When your toy is worn out, throw it away and make a new one. It won't cost a penny.

GOOD DOGS ARE MADE, NOT BORN

It is no accident when an adult dog behaves correctly while left alone.

If your dog has become a nuisance or has forgotten his good manners, don't give up. All dog owners find it necessary to do a little retraining every few months to prevent their forgetful pet from acquiring and keeping bad habits.

Many times between six and eighteen months your dog will think up some mischief that will really shock you! Don't be upset. This is normal for your growing pup. Like a growing child, your pet is getting bigger, smarter, meaner, and sweeter. In other words, he's learning how far he can go and how much he can do before you stop him. He's going to dig, bark, tease, beg, jump joyously, and cry piteously. All this to test you, his beloved owner.

Look at him now. So innocent, so sweet, talking to you with such heartrending love in his eyes.

It's hard to remember that this is the same dog that dumped the wastebasket all over the kitchen floor and ate a package of stolen cookies while you were away yesterday. To top it all, after you spanked and put him outside, he refused to come when you called.

Don't worry! There's small chance of your dog becoming a destructive adult dog if you take time to retrain when necessary. He should also have adequate chew toys and be taught while still young what he may and may not do.

ACCEPTABLE CHEW TOYS

When you leave your dog alone, be sure the dog always has adequate chew toys and bones. A big knuckle bone, hard rubber balls or tennis balls, along with the excellent rawhide chew toys, many times will be adequate.

I had a bit of luck with Libra when I realized how much she loved large rawhide chew bones. Since she's a big, active dog who roams the house instead of sleeping while we are gone, she and Kilty both get a rawhide bone to chew just before we leave. I only do this when we are leaving for four hours or more.

Upon returning, after praising their good behavior, I remove the bones and reward the dogs with small doggie treats. I do not give the dogs their bones again until the next time they must stay alone. I figure a bone keeps Libra occupied for at least two hours. By limiting the use of the bones, both dogs seem to feel it is a big treat to have Mom leave the house so they can have a good chew.

This is not a complete solution for working people but it will help if you too give a safe bone to your dog twice a week. At the same time rotate your dog's other toys to keep a little novelty in your pet's daily life.

CHEWING—DIFFERENT DISCIPLINE FOR OLDER DOGS

Unfortunately it may be necessary for you to use stronger, more effective discipline on the older dog. A little Tabasco sauce dabbed on forbidden objects will discourage a puppy, but many times an older chewer will devour the Tabasco without batting an eye. That same active dog can strip the stuffing from a sofa while you are running to the store to pick up something for dinner.

There are solutions other than getting rid of a destructive dog. Try this method first and do all you can to change your dog's bad habits.

The first step in retraining your growing dog to behave when left alone is isolation in a small area. You cannot dog-proof the whole house and you cannot teach the dog unless he is under control. A kitchen is an ideal spot in which to leave the dog alone.

For a few weeks it will be necessary to dog-proof the room while you are away. Before leaving the dog alone, remove all tempting, chewable objects such as wastebaskets, towels, books and food. Put a few dabs of Tabasco sauce on the legs of any furniture that the dog might enjoy chewing. If you know that the dog will eat Tabasco sauce, mix it with vinegar, pepper and other hot spices.

There are some commercial products on the market which might help. One product is called "No Bite." It is used to prevent horses from chewing their stalls. It's also effective in discouraging dogs from chewing.

Alum may be purchased in any pharmacy, and it is effective. Don't use too much or the dog will get a stomach ache. Alum should be mixed with water to make a paste and spread where necessary.

Ask a veterinarian for the preparation that he uses to prevent animals from ripping out their stitches. The medicine is effective and tastes terrible. I put this type of medicine on bread and left it on the table to cure Libra of stealing food.

Whatever medicine you try, be cautious, check it out with your vet and use sparingly. *Always read all instructions and use as directed.*

After you have dog-proofed the room, you are ready to start your retraining lessons. Begin by leaving your dog alone in the home for about 15 minutes. When you return be sure to enthusiastically praise his good behavior.

Gradually lengthen the dog's time alone until he will stay content for a full day with no damage to the room. This will take time and effort but at this point you have almost won the battle.

If you are away all day during the week, start this teaching program on Friday evening and continue all weekend. Forget all of the fun you'll be missing. This weekend could change your life and your attitude toward your "bad dog." It's a great help if every adult in the house helps and shares this experience.

TRAINING WITH BALLOONS

There is always something exciting going on in a houseful of children and pets. A good example was close to home, in fact, at my next door neighbor's. Rick and Debbie were busy raising two pre-schoolers and one young, half-trained golden retriever named Clark.

One evening Rick walked into the house and saw Debbie sitting on the living room floor blowing up balloons. Their son Stephen and dog Clark raced about the room chasing the multi-colored balloons, adding chaos to the occasion.

"Anyone for a party?" quipped Rick.

"No such luck," gasped Debbie, as she tied another knot. "These are going to help me teach Clark not to jump up and scratch the back door."

With these few remarks, she continued to inflate and tie the balloons.

In a short time, Clark bit into his first balloon and recoiled at the unfamiliar explosion. As the balloon broke, Debbie said "no" in a firm voice. Repeating the action, Debbie popped balloons with a pin, saying "no" each time the noise occurred.

Before long, Clark decided he did not like the game, the noise, nor the balloons, and ran into the other room.

Next, Debbie tied a string to each balloon and taped three rows of them onto the lower half of the battle-scarred back door.

Clark, each time forgetting the noise of the exploding spheres, jumped on the door, only to be rebuffed by the threatening sound. Before long he decided not to scratch on the door, and soon learned a soft whine or bark was the magical way to make the door open.

Two weeks later, Debbie, confident that the family pet would no longer scratch to get in, repainted the damaged surface of the door.

Clark, meanwhile, was delighted to receive praise instead of discipline each time he whined or barked at the door.

BALLOONS AS IMAGINATIVE DETERRENTS

Balloons may be pushed against a strip of wide, double-sided sticky tape which you have applied to any hard or soft surface, such as a table leg or sofa cushion. This will keep the dog where he belongs while you are away. Balloons can be taped or tied to many surfaces, and used as far as your imagination will stretch.

Sticky tape is often effective alone, since pets shun putting their feet anywhere sticky. You can put a small amount of pepper onto the tape as an added repellent.

TO DISCOURAGE WANDERING DOGS: Balloons on one occasion were intended to deter a large black mutt that prowled through my back yard during the night. Late one evening, I tied a handful of balloons onto my garbage can cover. After all, I didn't want to hurt the dog, just discourage his marauding ways.

Well, the next day, much to my surprise, the balloons were gone and so was the garbage. I later learned that the garbage collector had taken the balloons home to his children, and as he thanked me, confided that none of his other customers had been so thoughtful. I left the man and called the neighbor, laughing while I told her the tale. She graciously agreed to keep her pet at home.

TO PROTECT THE NESTING BIRDS: Another time, I decorated the mid-section of the pole on my bird feeder with assorted shapes and colors of balloons to discourage the neighborhood cats, dog, and squirrels from disturbing the nesting birds. I attracted more than the usual amount of neighborhood children on that occasion.

A beautiful mama cardinal built a nest and raised her young in a small tree in our yard. I'm sure she was confident that I would care for her and her brood. The nest was accessible to just about everyone and everything. It didn't bother the cardinal a bit to spend the summer surrounded by brightly colored balloons, which fortunately kept the curious animals away.

Although the balloons near the nest occasionally broke, they were easily replaced. Being a foster mother is not easy and I was relieved but a little sad to the see the last baby bird leave the nest.

I have never heard of a pet being hurt by balloons. I think it would be rare to have this happen. Dogs are accident-prone, simply because they put everything in their mouths. It is always wise to use caution and common sense with balloons and any other training method.

THERE'S A TRICK TO "SIT UP" TRAINING

I wrote in my newspaper column about the ''food on the nose'' trick that our dogs enjoy performing. It was nice to hear that many readers taught their dogs the trick and both pets and owners had great fun.

At the same time, several dog owners mentioned that they were having difficulty teaching their dog to "sit up."

Until a few years ago I would have laughed at anyone who couldn't teach their dog this simple trick. I have owned Poodles, Boxers, Beagles and assorted hunting dogs as well as a half-dozen mutts. Everyone of them learned to sit up. Then I bought our Sheltie Kilty.

Now, anyone would think that a dog who shakes hands, balances food on her nose, works by hand signals and can catch anything thrown to her would be able to sit up.

Our son Kelly had tried to teach Kilty to sit up when she was young, but the dog was neither cooperative nor interested. The family decided that the dog had a round bottom, like a roly-poly toy, and forgot all about it.

After hearing my reader's comments, I decided to teach both Libra and Kilty to "sit up."

The first week of teaching was uneventful. Libra, fondly called Lumpy by the family because her front end never seems to know what her back end is knocking over, fell over each time she tried to sit up. "Ole round bottom" disdainfully refused to lift one paw.

Exactly one month later both dogs sat up, held a tidbit on their noses, then tossed and caught the food on command.

How did I do it? I'll tell you exactly how I taught the trick and guarantee you also can teach your dog to sit up, if you are insistent and persistent.

Take your dog to the corner of a room. Leave a training collar and leash on the dog. If the floor where you are training is slippery, put down a small rug for your dog to sit upon.

Place the dog with his back to the corner of the walls and have him "sit." Now say "sit up" and at the same time put your left hand under his chin, pushing the dog up and back into the corner. If the dog resists, pull the leash taut above the head with the right hand. The walls will support the dog's body from the sides as well as the back thus giving him confidence. While the dog is sitting up say "stay." A few seconds later release the dog with an "OK, good dog," and allow him to relax.

Repeat this step of the training five times, release your pet and give him a treat. At this time do not give your dog the food until after he has performed. If you hold the food over your dog's head to make him sit up, he may later refuse to sit up until he has seen the treat. This is canine "blackmail."

Once the dog has learned to sit up in the corner, move him to a side wall, where he will be braced from the back. Now he will learn to balance himself sideways. Next move the dog away from the wall but hold the leash ready to help steady him if he starts to fall.

I used this method to teach Libra to sit up and since she cooperated and enjoyed the lessons, it didn't take her long to learn to balance her long back. Kilty still stubbornly refused to sit up unless I held her in place.

At this point drastic methods were required, Obviously nothing but bribery would work and Kilty's greed for food did her in.

I usually feed the dogs once a day, in the evening. Since it is a common practice for kennels to skip one meal a week, I omitted one evening meal for both dogs without feeling guilty.

The next morning I sat in the kitchen with a dish of dry kibbles. I showed one kibble, but did not hold it over the dog's head, then I said, "sit up." Libra immediately sat up and received the food.

Six kibbles later, Kilty swallowed her pride and sat up.

Happily, once Kilty decided to sit up, she graciously showed no ill will toward her trainer. In fact, now she seems to enjoy doing her trick as much as Libra does.

"COME WHEN CALLED"—FOR YOUR GROWING DOG

There is no doubt that teaching "come when called" takes more work than any other training exercise. It must be practiced daily and you must continually stay alert and try new techniques. *Do not allow your dog off the leash out of doors unless you are positive he will "come when called."* It is permissible to allow the dog to be free in a fenced area since you will be able to catch the dog should he refuse to come.

Continue working with your dog on a rope while teaching him to "come." As he improves, allow the dog more and more rope, but insist he come as soon as you call.

I like to use a roll of twine when working on the "come." It's cheap, lightweight and easy to handle. If your dog pulls extra hard you may prefer a heavier rope.

Sit on the ground in a large open area. If possible find a place where the rope won't tangle around trees or shrubs. Allow your dog to wander, then suddenly say your dog's name with the command "come." The dog's name is used only to get his attention. It is never a command in itself. After using the dog's name, you must then give a command telling him what you want him to do. In this case you want him to "come," fast. If he fails to come immediately, give a short, sharp jerk on the leash to get him in motion. Repeat your command as you pull the dog toward you and really mean it.

Always praise your dog when he comes to you. As the training proceeds you will know when your dog is ready to work off leash. Start with short lessons, and always end with some command you know the dog performs well. You can then honestly praise him and finish your work with a little play.

There will be times when your dog misbehaves while working off leash. Put the leash back on the dog and insist he work correctly. Try off leash again but always enforce your control by immediately putting the dog on the leash when he is bad. He is learning that good behavior leads to freedom and fun.

There are dogs that absolutely refuse to come when you call. Whether they are flighty, dumb, or just plain stubborn, you will have to get the lesson into their heads. It can be done, I guarantee. You may have to work longer and harder, but don't give up.

CRICKET THE TERRIBLE

I once owned a little Wire-Haired Terrier named "Cricket." She was the cutest, smartest, most stubborn dog I've ever owned. She knew her duty but carried it too far. Everytime I opened the front door, she rushed out to challenge the world. She was so fast her feet cleared four steps to land on the lower sidewalk.

I tried to solve this problem by putting a rope on the dog before I opened the door. It really worked. Everytime she had the rope on her collar, Cricket behaved. But each time someone forgot and opened the door without first attaching her rope, the dog bolted out of the house.

This was too much nonsense with an active family going in and out of the house.

I finally solved the problem by attaching a strong light-weight fishline to Cricket's training collar. I knew she wouldn't notice because we often removed or put on the collar.

The time had come. I tied the twenty-foot line to the inside doorknob, slipped the collar on the dog and had Carrie go around the house to ring the front doorbell.

The bell rang, the dog barked, I opened the door, the dog bolted down the steps and I called her just as she hit the end of the fishline.

She was going so fast that she got jerked over on her back.

I walked out, picked her up, brought her in the house and sympathized with her. After all, as far as she knew, I hadn't done a thing.

After four lessons Cricket still bolted out of the door, but from then on she stopped just short of the terrible spot. Once she halted, I could get her attention easily. Each time I called she dutifully turned and came back into the house.

Our relationship improved a great deal after Cricket and I both gained knowledge from that lesson.

On the outside, ordeals like this seem to show that only the dog gained from the experience. This isn't true. I learned the most important secret there is in dog training:

As humans, we are smarter than our dogs. When we have a problem, we have the ability to find a solution.

CLEVER PETS CAN TALK

Teaching your dog to perform a few tricks along with his basic obedience is always fun and rewarding. We all have the feeling that any dog can sit and lie down but how many dogs can "carry" "play dead" or "speak" on command.

When Libra was about eight months old, she was already barking at strangers so we decided to teach her to speak on command.

I always have taught my dogs to bark when I say "speak." This time after a family discussion, we decided not to use the word "speak" when we wanted the dog to bark. Instead, we would use the word "say" to invite the dog to bark.

This idea may sound a little crazy at first but if you think about it for a while, you will understand our reasoning.

By teaching the dog that the key word to bark is "say," we can then use the word in ordinary conversation such as "say thank you," "say hello," "say goodbye." This sounds much more conversational than to always say "speak" to the dog.

Our only problem so far is that I have a hard time remembering to use "say" instead of "speak." Since the younger members of the family are having no trouble with this, I'm sure that their persistence offsets my few mistakes.

If your dog is a natural watchdog and barks whenever he hears a noise this lesson will be easy to teach. When the dog starts to bark, loudly say the word ''say'' to him and praise the dog. You also may have to tell the dog to be ''quiet'' if he barks too long. Your barker will soon learn to speak on command and you will have no trouble teaching him.

If you have one of the many breeds that are not inclined to bark, you will have to use a little persuasion. Food is always the best way to a dog's heart. If your dog is a good eater and seems always hungry, he can be taught to speak by showing him food. Use the word ''say'' but do not give him food until he barks at your command. Later pretend you have food in your hand, give your command ''say,'' and praise him when he obeys.

After a short time do not pretend you have anything for him to eat, but give your command in the same tone that you used when you were using food as a reward.

Once you have taught your dog the trick of speaking on command, you can actually carry on a conversation with him. "Say, do you want a dog bone?" or, "Say, who do you think will be the next president?"

People will be absolutely astounded by your intelligent dog's answers.

PLANTS AND PETS

He was a delightful puppy, just eight weeks old and begging for a home. The couple had lost their old dog a few months before and the pain and emptiness of their loss persisted.

It was mutual love at first sight as the wiggling, joyful pup went to his new home carefully wrapped in a blanket.

Within a week the puppy was accustomed to his new surroundings, the soft warm bed, and the loving hands which gave both joy and discipline. Only occasionally did he slip out of the kitchen to explore the rest of the house. His greatest joy was chasing a small ball.

One day his owner came into the kitchen, called the pup, and rolled the ball. The pup stayed quietly in his bed, the little tail wagging, the bright eyes soulful and pleading.

Immediately alert that there was something wrong, the owner searched for the reason the puppy was sick. On the floor of the living room lay a half chewed leaf of a philodendron plant.

After a quick dash to the veterinarian's office, this story had a happy ending. Three days later the puppy went home alive and well.

Many such episodes as this true story do not end as happily. Lengthy paralysis, emotional trauma, expensive medical bills, and sometimes death are the result of dogs and cats eating poisonous plants.

House plants are currently the rage of the country. During a long cold winter, plants are a soothing promise of spring. But how many of us know that a vast number of beautiful and often fragrant plants are poisonous and can be lethal if an animal or human nibbles on a leaf or stem.

Consider the bulbs of crocus, daffodils, iris and hyacinth being set in our gardens in the fall. Nearly all bulbs are dangerous if eaten. If you have a dog that likes to dig, it would be safer to put a small fence around the planted area.

While you are outside check your yard and crush any toadstools you find. They are extremely dangerous, yet sometimes quite attractive to a dog.

Cats and dogs crave greenery. Remember seeing your pet eat grass? In the winter when there is nothing available outside, household plants make a good substitute in the eyes of your pet.

Oleander, philodendron, dumb cane, elephant ear, rhododendron, ivy, castorbean and jatropha are all dangerous if leaf or stem is eaten. Many outside plants from the South are now being raised as indoor plants in the North. Poinsettia, sweet pea and lily of the valley can be fatal if eaten in large quantities.

A concerned garden shop owner warns, "Many innocent plants become dangerous, if eaten after they have been sprayed with insecticide or fungicide. Plant medications such as these, as well as leaf polishes, can remain potent for up to four weeks when applied to plants."

Often a little Tabasco sauce dabbed on the edge of the planter and on a few leaves will repel your cat or dog. Tabasco sauce will not damage a firm leaf such as philodendron and, of course, will not harm your pet.

The vast assortment of hanging planters now available will also make it easy for you and your pets to live comfortably and safely in a house filled with beautiful plants.

"TAKE" "HOLD" "GIVE"

It is encouraging to find that many people take the time to teach their dogs correct behavior in the home and yard.

On the other hand, it is disappointing that the same people fail to go one step farther and teach their dog tricks that will entertain both the dog and family.

The average dog is capable of learning a tremendous vocabulary, and will associate most words with an appropriate action. While your dog does not rationalize like a human, he does learn through repetition. He enjoys the very repetition that we humans find boring. For example, chasing a ball or stick is never tiring to our pet, but we mortals soon say "enough" and walk away.

Once your dog has learned some basic obedience such as come, sit and down, he will easily learn to "take" "hold" and "carry" an object, then "give" to you on command. Carrying an object is sheer pleasure for almost every dog. Surely you have noticed how eagerly your dog will return to you with something in his mouth, yet lag and drag when you call him at other times.

There are two great advantages gained once your dog will "take" "hold" and "give." The greatest being that with the simple word "give," you have absolute control over everything your dog puts into his mouth. No more wrestling with your dog to remove a harmful or forbidden article. With the command "give," you will quickly have the object dropped into your hand.

The other benefit of course is fun, fun, fun.

SMART DOGS "CARRY"

Let's teach your dog to carry. This trick is so easy to teach that even an older dog will learn it easily.

Roll a newspaper and fasten it with masking tape or several rubber bands. Sit your dog in a corner with his back to the wall so he will not move away from you.

Kneel beside the dog with the rolled newspaper in your right hand. Put your left hand over or under the dog's nose or jaw and open his mouth by applying pressure on the sides of the mouth with the thumb and fingers.

Be sure that you press at the back of the mouth where there is loose skin. As you open the mouth, hold the dog's lips over his back teeth so if he bites down it will pinch his skin instead of your hand.

Command the dog to "take" and place the newspaper in his mouth. He will try to spit it out, but hold it firmly in his mouth saying "hold."

Now, as you make the dog hold the newspaper tell him what a good dog he is.

After the dog has held the paper a few seconds, tell him to "give" and remove the newspaper. Say "OK" or "all right" to let him know that the lesson is over and praise his wonderful performance.

Repeat this exercise until the dog will open his mouth and take the newspaper on command. Be sure to use the three key words "take" "hold" and "give" and offer frequent praise.

When your dog holds the paper until you tell him he can release it, you are ready for the next step.

Fasten your dog's leash onto his collar. Tell him to "take" and "hold" then begin to walk slowly forward. If the dog tries to drop the paper while walking, use a stern voice and at the same time reach down and make the dog hold the paper. Reassure him with lots of praise while walking.

It will require only a lesson or two to give the dog the idea to "hold" while walking with you. Now you and your dog can have lots of fun playing the game of "carry."

"FETCH THE PAPER"

How would you like that smart dog of yours to fetch your slippers? Maybe you would like him to bring in the newspaper every night?

Put the leash on your dog and act as if you are going to have fun. Don't bother to make the dog heel, just happily jog outside to the spot where your newspaper is usually dropped by the paperboy. Tell your dog to "sit" as you pick up the paper. Put it into the dog's mouth with the commands "take" and "hold." Keep the dog on the leash until he has carried the paper inside the house. Once inside say "give" and praise his performance.

As you progress with this trick, increase your dog's vocabulary by adding the words "fetch" and "paper."

Once you have taught your dog to fetch the paper, he will easily learn to fetch or carry anything you would like. In fact, that is just what I once did when we had a long illness in the family. We lived in a two-story house, so running up the stairs to the sick room became a tiring ordeal. In desperation one day I put some small objects in a paper bag and sent the dog upstairs with it. She ran into the right room because the sick room was the only one occupied. This was so successful that I found a small basket with a handle for her to carry.

It was fun for the whole family to see how happily the dog carried out her important task. She delivered notes, pencils, magazines and, of course, the evening newspaper.

"ON YOUR RUG"

Teaching your dog that there are times when you are too busy to give it attention is essential to having a peaceful home.

Even the most affectionate owners do not want their dog to jump on them, or run across the clean floor when the dog has a wet coat or muddy paws. The answer to these and many other problems is quickly solved if you teach your dog to go to his rug and stay there until you say he may leave.

This is an easy lesson to teach your house pet and few dogs resent going to their rug, if it is placed in an area where the dog feels he is still with the family.

Since the kitchen is usually the center of activity, it's the ideal spot to put the dog's rug. An area near the back door, away from the working area is also acceptable for both you and your dog.

To teach your dog to go "on your rug" simply take him to the rug and say "on your rug" each time. While on his rug, it is a good idea to give the dog an occasional tidbit and lots of praise for a good performance. If the dog leaves the rug before you give permission, immediately

take him back and repeat the commands "on your rug" and "stay." Always give praise when the dog obeys your commands. Start with a short stay on the rug and gradually make it a little longer.

Once your dog has learned to go to the rug and stay, teach him to take all food to the rug before eating. The dog will learn this lesson even quicker because food from a loving hand is a pleasure.

Use a tidbit large enough to prevent the dog from eating before reaching the rug. A large milk bone is ideal. Open the dog's mouth and give him the food. At the same time say "on your rug" and hold the mouth closed with one hand making the dog carry the food.

Firmly grasp the collar with the other hand and lead your dog to his rug.

When on the rug tell your dog how great he is and allow your pet to eat the tidbit.

If you practice this lesson about three times a day, it will not be long before your dog will immediately take any hand-given food to the rug to eat.

You will not believe how convenient it is to have your dog go "to his rug" until you have tried it. No more tripping over your happy canine while fixing dinner. No more begging while the family is enjoying dinner. No more spots on the carpet from dropped food. And no more muddy feet all over you and the clean floor.

CONTROL DOG'S BARKING

The bark of a dog is not merely noise. To him it is a form of expression.

The vocal expressions of a dog show great variety. A dog can bark in many different ways and can vary the intensity, rhythm and frequency. A dog can keep the bark it makes constant or stop abruptly. The sound can be raised or lowered. As if the bark weren't enough, the dog can also howl, grunt, yelp, whine, snarl, bay, moan and wail. Few animals other than man can express the way they feel in as many ways as the dog.

Regardless of how enjoyable barking is to a dog, it is a pain to his owners and a nuisance to the neighbors.

If you teach your dog to control his barking when he is young, he will learn self-discipline and you will prevent having a neurotic barker. Of course you want your dog to bark to warn you of an unusual noise or a stranger lurking about, but he must learn to stop the barking after he has given the alert. Many dogs do not bark as a warning until eight to twelve months. Don't worry if your dog is just a lover. He will soon learn to tell friend from enemy.

When training a young pup, place your short rope on his collar and let him drag it around the house. He won't notice the rope and you will be able to catch and control him. When he barks to alert you, let him bark once or twice and tell him he's a good dog. Then use the command "quiet." Be firm when you tell him "quiet" and at the same time give his rope a jerk to startle him. Insist that he stop the noise immediately, and praise him the minute he becomes quiet. Be sure you are consistent with your discipline every time he barks.

FIRM DISCIPLINE STOPS BARKING

As your dog gets older and barks or howls for no good reason, walk up to him and close your hand around his muzzle forcefully. Hold his mouth closed and command him to be "quiet." If he tries to break away and bark, you will have to be more firm and forceful. Hold his mouth shut and snap your finger sharply across the dog's nose, again commanding him to be "quiet." *Once he has stopped the noise, and is silent, praise him to teach him he will always receive praise when he obeys you.*

Even an older dog can and should learn to be quiet in the home. These two methods, the rope jerk and holding the muzzle, if done consistently, will correct the dog's bad habit, regardless of age.

When your dog is outside and barking you will have a more difficult problem controlling him, but don't be discouraged. It can be done. You can stop the nuisance barking but once again it takes determination, constant watchfulness and discipline.

If your dog is tied outside, it will be easy for you to catch him to enforce your "no bark" rule. When your dog is in a fenced-in area running free you will need to have a drag rope on him or you will never catch him when he barks. Use the same method of discipline that you used inside the house: jerking the collar, holding the muzzle, and snapping the nose. At the same time insist that he be "quiet." Praise him again when he stops the noise. Before long you should be able to yell "quiet" out the door and enjoy the peaceful silence.

Some dogs become neurotic barkers and further discipline is needed to make them obey your command to be "quiet." A water hose turned on the dog in the summer will usually deter even the chronic barker. A sharp, hard, quick slap under the chin will also discourage your dog.

No matter what method you use, no amount of work will be effective in training your dog if you are not consistent yourself, and insist that every member of your family be the same.

If you find you cannot make the necessary effort to train

your dog to be quiet, then do not leave him outside alone. If necessary you may have to take him out on his leash four or five times a day. The rest of the time keep him inside the house where his barking will not disturb your neighbors.

PACK ANIMALS NEED LEADERSHIP

If your dog roamed wild and free, he would live with a pack of other dogs under the direction of a strong canine leader. Since your dog has no pack leader, he needs and looks to you for direction and leadership. Don't let him down!

You have taught your dog "sit," "stay," "down" and "come," plus other key words. Together with the word "no" you now have your dog under control and quite liveable. Yet there is more training to do.

When you feel tired and discouraged try to remember that the year or eighteen months of hard work put into training your dog will give you ten to fifteen years of happiness with an obedient companion. He will repay you by guarding you, your family, and your home.

CLASSY TRICKS FOR CLASSY DOGS

Occasionally I like to write about tricks that almost any dog can perform.

My family, like others, enjoys showing off our dogs when guests visit.

The most enjoyable trick our dogs perform is balancing a bit of food on their noses, holding it, then throwing the treat into the air and catching it on command before it touches the ground.

Surprisingly, though this trick sounds difficult to teach, it's fun and very easy on the instructor. Dogs, of course, love learning this trick since it involves food. As any dog owner knows, the way to a dog's heart is with food.

This trick should be taught before the dog has eaten its daily meal while it is good and hungry. Arm yourself with a supply of crackers or dry dog kibbles. Do not use a large or heavy treat such as a dog biscuit. A small cracker is great to use if your dog likes the taste. They are flat and will balance nicely on the dog's nose.

I usually wait to teach this trick until my dog is fairly well obedience-trained and is about a year old. The reason why I wait is that the dog must sit quietly and hold its head perfectly still to successfully balance the food. This requires obedience and maturity from the dog.

It's best to work in the kitchen while teaching your dog this trick since the dog may miss catching the food a number of times.

Place your dog in a sit position, facing you. You will be comfortable sitting in a chair with the dog's nose close to your lap. Grasp the dog's jaw firmly underneath with your left hand. At the same time tell the dog to "hold" or "stay." Place the treat on the top of the dog's nose, close to the end and repeat the "hold" or "stay" command. Keep the jaw immobile for a few seconds repeating "hold" and "good dog." as you release your hold on the dog's jaw say "OK" and remove the treat.

PRACTICE, PATIENCE, PRAISE TEACHES TRICK

Practice this first part of the trick for a few days. Praise the dog and give the treat each time it holds its head quietly until released.

Occasionally even the best trained dog will move its head and allow the food to fall to the floor. It is very important that you say "no" and remove the food before the dog gobbles it down. The dog must understand that the only way it will get the snack is by doing the trick correctly. After the dog has learned to hold its nose immobile, you may teach the rest of the trick.

This time, as you release your hold on the dog's jaw, say "OK" but don't move the food. Pat the dog sharply under the jaw to snap his head up a little. The food will fly and the dog will try to catch the treat. Praise the dog for its effort but do not allow it to eat the food from the floor.

Your dog will not catch the food the first few tries, but it won't take long to realize that the tasty snack will fall, and the dog will make every effort to catch the food before it reaches the floor.

Before long, your dog will toss its head when you say "OK" and catch the food as it falls opposite its mouth. This is a catchy trick and very impressive to watch.

If your dog has learned to sit up, have it do this trick while in the "up" position. Sitting up while performing is real class in the world of dogs. Don't worry if your dog doesn't catch the food all of the time. With practice it will learn to hold, and catch anything you put on its nose and the dog will love this bit of fun.

PETS CAN HAVE EMOTIONAL PROBLEMS

One day your dog is well-behaved, mature and clean in its personal habits. A day later, while guests sit in your living room, this same well-mannered dog wets on the carpet with no warning and no indication that it wishes to go out of doors. What's more, after flagrantly disobeying the rules of a well-trained dog, it trots over and wags its tail at you as if nothing were wrong.

This is an embarrassing, frustrating situation. You yell, smack and isolate the offender while apologizing to your guests. Inside, you are disappointed to despair. The dog has misbehaved before. Why? To the owner it is a return to the disagreeable moments of toilet training.

In virtually all cases, what the dog is experiencing is not a loss of memory, but a symptom of either an emotional or physical problem.

It's easy to learn if the dog has kidney or bladder problems by consulting a veterinarian. Dogs having kidney or bladder problems are usually more than six or seven years old and drink large amounts of water. They usually urinate frequently.

When there is no physical problem, owners must assume the dog is emotionally upset.

NEW BABY IN HOME

A new baby in the home definitely is a threat to a pet which has monopolized all of its owner's love and time.

Most dogs and cats do not appreciate even a new puppy or kitten in the house. The ugly horns of jealousy rise and the senior pet plans retaliation.

What better way to pay everyone back than misbehave under the guise of innocence.

Animals are amazing masters of retaliation, although they don't always go as far as soiling. Many times their rage or jealousy is demonstrated by climbing on forbidden furniture, nipping, refusing to eat, or ignoring previously obeyed commands.

Owners don't have to bring a new member into the house to rouse their pet's ire. The absence of a much loved member of the family can be devastating to a pet. A change in environment, such as moving to a new home or apartment, is a traumatic experience for both human and animal.

Leave pets in a boarding kennel for a few weeks and they'll walk into the house and wet on the floor. "Desertion by my owner must be punished," thinks our canine pet.

HELP FOR THE FRUSTRATED PET

Once the reason for a dog's poor behavior is learned, corrections can begin immediately.

If loneliness or jealousy is the cause, extra affection, a few treats and firm discipline will set the dog back on the straight and narrow. Above all do not ignore the situation, or the pet's behavior will get worse. It wants attention.

To correct irresponsible wetting, place a four or five foot long rope on the dog's collar. Tie the dog near a chair, table or wherever you are when at home. While away from the house, confine the dog to one room if necessary. Generally the dog will not wet while you are away. It wants your reaction.

Be firm if the dog starts to wet in the house. Say "no, no" and rush it outside. When it performs outside, praise the good behavior. This retraining usually will be successful within two weeks if you are consistent with your discipline.

When finally allowing the dog its freedom, watch it carefully for any signs of relapse. If it repeats the poor behavior, start with the rope again and continue training for a few more weeks.

Although it is necessary to be firm with the dog, try to be compassionate and remember it is upset and confused. Poor manners are the only method it has to communicate with you and tell you of its sorrow.

At all times give your pet extra love, attention and consistent discipline. Your reward will be a mature, happy, loving companion.

Part 3

Home Health Care

THE LEGEND OF ST. ROCH AND HIS DOG

During the 13th century, France was pestered by the plague. Death and illness were everywhere. In the province of Languedoc, St. Roch (who was born with the sign of the cross on his chest) ministered to peasants and nobility alike, giving aid, comfort and faith to the sick and needy. The saintly monk was always accompanied by his little dog.

In his zeal to help others, St. Roch eventually became exhausted and was stricken with the plague. Feeling death near at hand, the monk managed to crawl out of the city to a nearby forest. There he found refuge under a large tree.

Knowing his master was dying, the dog went off in search of food. He soon discovered a castle where a nobleman was carousing with his friends. Entering the great hall, the dog boldly ran to the table, snatched a loaf of bread and dashed out of the room. Day after day St. Roch's dog returned to the castle, seized a loaf of bread and ran off.

One day the nobleman followed the dog to see what he did with the food. He had not gone far before he discovered the old man and his dog. The loyal pet had dropped the bread at his master's feet, then lain beside his beloved friend, to lick his sores and keep the holy man warm.

The nobleman was so moved by the saint's holiness and the dog's devotion that he carried the saint to his castle and cared for him until he was well. The nobleman then forsook his self-indulgence, gave away his wealth and devoted his life to the service of God.

Thus the deeds of St. Roch who gave everything he had to God and his fellowman, and his faithful dog who gave everything he could to his God called man, have gone down in legend for almost 700 years.

THAT SKILLFUL INTRUDER—THE COMMON FLEA

Did you know that one little flea will bite your pet on the average of 25 times in one hour? Two fleas mean twice the discomfort. You can imagine the havoc a whole family of fleas can wreak upon your unsuspecting animal in just a short time.

The flea's constant movement and biting causes itching and irritation that can make your pet so uncomfortable it

will be unable to rest. In addition, flea bites and the scratching they prompt can cause infections that require expensive treatment.

Since the flea lives on blood, a severe flea infestation can cause a pet to suffer from anemia, and cause weight loss and general deteriorating health.

If fleas weren't such dangerous and irritating little critters, one could almost admire their ability to survive. Fleas breed anywhere and everywhere. They love carpets and can survive and breed in the deep pile all year round. Outside, the yard and garden are also perfect breeding spots. Even if you never allow your pets outside, fleas will find their way to them. They can come on you or your clothing, or simply invade your home by jumping through doors and screened windows.

In warmer climates, fleas are a constant problem; while only the hardiest of fleas can survive the cold winter weather in the northern states. Regardless of where you live, after a few weeks of warm weather, the flea population literally explodes. That's why flea control should start early in the summer and continue throughout the warm fall months, even in the cold weather states.

Effective flea control includes removing the insects from both the animal and its environment. In fact, it's cruel to allow your household pets out of doors in the summer without adequate protection from flea infestation.

Spraying yards and gardens with a good yard and kennel spray, and repeating the treatment as often as directed on the container, is one effective flea control method. But one weapon alone will not win the war. It's also necessary to use either an effective flea spray or flea powder routinely or to put a flea collar on your dog and cat. If you have more than one pet, each must be treated since fleas can easily jump from one pet to the other.

You can increase the effectiveness of a spray or powder by wrapping your pet in a large blanket or towel for about 20 minutes after applying the insecticide. The cover will insure that the fleas don't simply jump off the animal before the poison has a chance to work. Do take care, however, to protect the pet's nose and eyes from the insecticide and keep its face open to fresh air during treatment. When you remove the wrapping you may be surprised at the number of dead fleas you'll find on the towel and on the animal's fur.

It's almost impossible to control fleas in most areas

114

without the help of insecticides, but if you treat the environment—spray the yard and the carpets and furniture in your home—you may be able to avoid using insecticides directly on the pet. Regular use of a flea comb may be all the extra protection your friend will need. A few pet owners have reported some success by feeding their animals brewer's yeast or tablets containing brewer's yeast as a means of repelling fleas. Frequent vacuuming, paying particular attention to corners and areas along the baseboards, is another effective, nonpoisonous method of flea control. Be sure to discard the dust bag frequently to keep it from becoming just another breeding ground for these hardy pests.

Certainly, the most popular method of flea control is flea collars. Collars are convenient, comparatively inexpensive and effective when used correctly. However there are a few possible dangers you should guard against.

THE FLEA COLLAR is damp when the package is first opened. Leave the collar in the opened package until it's dry—usually two days. Avoid touching the damp collar.

ONCE THE COLLAR is dry, snap it sharply to activate the repellent. Wipe the excess powder off the collar before placing it around the animal's neck and be sure to wash your hands after handling the collar.

THE COLLAR SHOULD be loose enough to allow you to slide two fingers between the collar and the pet's neck, but not so loose that the animal can slide it up and into its mouth. (This can happen and usually results in a very sick pet!)

CHECK THE PET'S skin underneath the collar periodically for any sign of skin irritation. If any redness or rash appears, remove the collar at once and consult your veterinarian.

CUT OFF THE extra length of collar. If your pet chews on the dangling collar, he may show signs of poisoning such as vomiting, diarrhea, and convulsions.

DO NOT PUT a flea collar on a very young pet. Kittens and puppies should be at least 12 weeks old before wearing a flea collar.

DO NOT WRAP a collar around your pet's neck more than once even if it is long enough to allow this.

DO NOT USE a dog flea collar on a cat. Use only collars specifically made for cats.

DO NOT USE a flea collar in combination with other insecticides such as shampoos, dips or powders—unless the procedure is specifically recommended by your veterinarian.

AVOID TOUCHING THE collar to your face when you handle your pet. Human skin will sometimes react to the insecticide, producing a rash that can last up to 90 days.

Certainly pet health care is at times inconvenient and expensive, however your efforts will be richly repaid with the affection you and your pet will share for many years.

EVEN "BEST FRIEND" NEEDS A BATH

At last I have found a practical use for my disposable dry cleaning bags. The soft pliable plastic makes a perfect cover-up to protect my clothes while I give my dogs a bath.

Just poke holes in the bag for your head and arms, slip it on and you are protected against water, soap and rinse splashes.

Brushing your dog to keep him clean and odor-free is important and beneficial. But since dogs don't sweat, there comes a time when brushing is no longer enough, and even you cannot stand to have your best friend around.

For many of the medium to short-haired breeds, dry shampoo or even brisk rubdowns with wet towels are effective for between-bath cleansing. Poodles and long-haired dogs require hours of brushing, along with frequent water baths.

Small dogs can be bathed comfortably in small basement tubs. Larger dogs will have to be bathed in the family bath tub.

There are many commercial shampoos available for every type of dog hair. Most of them are adequate, but expensive.

Here is a recipe for shampoo, given to me by a professional breeder. The shampoo is cheap, smells nice and can

117

be used for all breeds of dogs. In fact, it is an excellent shampoo for the entire family. It calls for 1/4 cup white vinegar, 1/4 cup glycerin (2 ounces purchased at the pharmacy) and 1 quart of pink liquid dishwasher detergent.

Put all ingredients in a clean gallon container, add water to the top and shake. You will be able to handle the gallon of shampoo better if you fill the detergent container and refill the smaller bottle when necessary.

This shampoo doesn't bother my dogs' eyes, but if you have trouble, use baby shampoo for your pet's face and head. Use the regular shampoo for the rest of the body. As a precaution put a few drops of mineral oil in his eyes to prevent soap irritation.

A dog with ears that stand up will appreciate it if you gently stuff a little cotton in each ear before bathing.

While filling the tub, pretend you are bathing a baby. The water temperature should be about 105 degrees F. You can test with your hand, but remember dogs and babies will feel more heat in their bath water than you feel with your hand. The rinse water should be a little cooler than the bath water.

Begin with the head and wash downward and backward. Your dog will need two good soapings followed by thorough rinses. Now is the time to make use of all your obedience work. Make the dog sit, lie and stand in the tub as you progress with the cleansing.

Put a bit of fragrant creme rinse in the final tub and your dog emerges clean, happy and sweet smelling. For white dogs a final rinse with a capful of laundry blueing will leave the coat glistening like snow.

TRIMMING YOUR DOG'S NAILS

After your dog's bath it's very important to check the dog's nails. They are clean and slightly softened by the bath water, making them easy to look over and file or trim, if needed. Nail trimming is a simple task, and absolutely essential for your dog's health. When neglected nails grow long and become crooked, splayed feet may result. This prevents the dog from walking correctly and is very painful for the pet. Splayed feet are similar to fallen arches in humans.

Many veterinarians and professional groomers charge

reasonable fees for nail trimming and you must either do it yourself, or pay to have it done. Here are some suggestions to help you get the job done as quickly as possible.

Dogs nails should be cut so they just clear the floor. Do not cut too short.

Try to set a schedule to trim your dog's nails once a week from the pup's earliest months. It is a good idea to schedule brushing, health check and nail trimming all together. If you work at grooming and nail trimming weekly, your dog will enjoy the attention and remain calm as he matures.

Household scissors shouldn't be used to trim a dog's nails. Specially designed nail trimmers can be bought in pet departments or pet stores. I like the nail trimmer that works like a guillotine. You insert the nail in a small hole and a razor sharp blade moves down and cuts the nail.

If your dog has white nails, you can see the blood line and trim just below it with little difficulty. When your dog has black nails, you have the problem of estimating where the blood line is. You had better cut just a little of the nail at a time. This is nerve-wracking and you are bound to cut too close sometimes. The bleeding can be stopped with a small amount of Moncel solution, silver nitrate, or styptic stick, which are available at any animal clinic, drug store or pet shop.

While cutting your dog's nails is the fastest method, there are other ways that are easier for both you and the dog. I prefer to use a metal file. For small dogs with softer nails, any hand file from the workshop will do. A larger dog will need the nails cut first, then filed to smooth the rough edges.

Years ago we solved our nail problem with our Boxer Heidi. We used our quarter-inch electric drill with coarse sandpaper discs to file her hard nails. You can buy differing grades of sandpaper to fit your needs.

A small grinding wheel is perfect to use on your dog's nails if you get the dog used to the noise and vibrations while he is young. There is no pain to the pup and with a little practice you can trim your dog's nails in just a few minutes.

As with teaching a young dog to accept being trimmed with an electric clipper, start by holding the pup and clipper and slowly help the dog to accept the motor noise. At the same time, talk to your pup while you pet him and give him treats. Within a short time the puppy will ignore the noise and you can carefully begin trimming, either nails or hair, with little resistance from your dog.

CARE OF THE EARS

Canine ears are sensitive, troublesome, and practically inaccessible. The most difficult type of ear to keep clean and free from infection is the drop ear. All hounds, spaniels, and poodles have heavy skinned, hair-laden drop ears.

The weight of the ear prevents air from circulating to

keep the ear canal dry. Moist warm conditions such as in a dog's ear are breeding grounds for ear infections, often called ear cankers.

The first symptom of ear trouble often is a slight, foul odor. Examination with a penlight usually will show redness as a sign of irritation in the ear canal.

Because the lining of the ear is delicate and easily injured, you should be aware of some of the probable causes of infection.

Dirt, wax and excessive hair will create an ideal condition for infection in the ear. Periodic cleansing will help. Carefully pull out the hairs in the ear a few at a time. This will not bother the dog. The hair you see deep in the ear canal is best left alone. Removing this hair with tweezers is dangerous, and unless done by a veterinarian can damage the ear.

Next, wash away all noticeable surface wax and dirt. Cotton balls, soft-stick Q-tips and acne pads are effective for this delicate area. Warm water, alcohol, or a little warm mineral oil, may also be used.

When bathing your dog, make it a regular routine to clean and carefully dry the dog's ears. Avoid using strong shampoos or dips with harsh chemicals as they can cause permanent damage.

There is a minute spider-like parasite called the otodectes mite which causes cankers in the ears of dogs, cats and even rabbits. Ear mites are a common cause of ear problems in canines. When ear mites are present, the affected

animal will shake his head, scratch, and hold the painful ear down. If the condition is severe enough the animal will become dizzy or walk in circles.

Tumors, another touchy ear problem, may appear at any time in a canine ear and will have to be diagnosed and treated by a veterinarian.

As with any health problem, ear infections should be diagnosed and treated by a skillful, well-trained vet. Certainly you can prevent many infections by cleanliness, taking precaution and protecting the ear against foreign objects.

Since many of our drop-eared dogs are hunters, it is sensible to check your dog's ears after a run in the field. Burrs, seeds, dirt and debris should be carefully removed before irritation sets in.

Although not recommended by all vets, there are antibiotic ear powders for cats and dogs which may be purchased in any pet supply department. These powders, if used every two or three weeks along with thorough ear cleansing, are quite effective in keeping the ears dry.

SHOPPING FOR A VETERINARIAN

Most pet owners are as genuinely concerned about choosing a good veterinarian as they are about choosing a good family practitioner. It's wise to start your pet with a veterinarian while the animal is very young because your pet should receive all necessary inoculations and at least one checkup each year.

How should you choose a veterinarian? What makes one vet better than another? Is a good personality important?

Here are some practical tips for pet owners.

The easiest and most direct method of finding the best vet for you is to talk about it with friends and acquaintances. You may also write to your State Veterinarian Medical Association for a list of animal doctors in your area.

Most reputable veterinarians are members of their state association and can take advantage of the educational courses offered. This helps them keep up to date with the latest developments in their field.

Once you have chosen a vet, make a visit to the office. One visit will tell many things. Are the facilities and staff clean? Is everyone helpful and kind in handling your animal? Do they really listen to what you have to say and honestly try to answer your questions? Is someone available day and night for an emergency? Are they willing to discuss the cost of specific services such as worming, neutering and shots?

Animal doctors, may specialize in large and small animals which would include horses and cows, or they may provide service to only small animals. Some vets specialize in a particular medical field such as dermatology, radiology or opthalmology.

Any reputable veterinarian will send clients to a specialist when necessary. In return, you should also feel free to consult another doctor if you are uncomfortable with the diagnosis or treatment of your pet. Please have the courtesy of talking your concern over with your vet before going to another doctor.

Occasionally you may be upset about the treatment, or worse, the death of your pet. If you feel that your veterinarian has behaved in an unethical or unscrupulous manner, you may inform your State Board of Veterinary Medicine which will investigate the situation. This is a serious step and should not be taken lightly. You should give yourself time to calm down, get over your grief and once again talk to your vet before considering such a measure.

Happily with proper exercise, good nutrition and loving care, most of us have pets who live long lives and maintain good health with only a yearly visit to a veterinarian.

TIMING CRUCIAL FOR VETERINARIAN

Knowing when to take your dog to the veterinarian is one of the most perplexing problems for the average dog owner.

If I take my dog to the doctor at the beginning of an illness, I am usually told that it's a little early to tell.

If I wait and take the dog when she is really sick, I'm told that I just made it, but with a little luck and a great deal of skill she might survive.

Tiring of this type of hit or miss diagnosis I have developed a list of "hurry to the vet" symptoms, and a list of "wait and see" symptoms that I have found useful. You may also find them helpful.

BREATHING DIFFICULTY: If the dog has been exercising vigorously, labored breathing is normal. If the dog frequently gasps for breath or pants after a short run you should be concerned. Your dog might have foreign matter in the lungs, an allergy or respiratory disease. Shortness of breath may be a result of insufficient oxygen to the heart. Heartworm, severe anemia or broken ribs all create a demand for more air. Don't wait! Take your dog to the vet immediately.

RUNNY EYES: If this is the only symptom the dog has, wash out his eyes twice a day with cotton balls and sterile water. Unless the eyes become bloodshot or have pus in the corners, I don't worry about the dog; the eyes usually clear in a few days. If other signs of illness develop with the eye problem, of course you must find out what the trouble is.

COUGHING: This is always serious enough to stay alert. If a cough persists for more than two days you must get the dog to a vet immediately. Coughing is nature's way of clearing the respiratory passages of obstruction. A cough could be a symptom of an allergy, pneumonia, kennel cough or an obstruction in the throat. Coughing should never be ignored.

VOMITING: Many people are so disgusted and angry with this unpleasant act that they forget that vomiting is a symptom of intestinal disorder. A light cold, eating spoiled food, or a stomach obstruction are among reasons the stomach rejects food. I usually stop all food for 24 hours if one of my dogs has a stomach upset. After 24 hours I give a very light meal and see if the dog retains the food. If he vomits again it is best to call the vet and discuss the problem.

SNEEZING: When sneezing is the only symptom I observe, I usually assume my dog has run into something that she is allergic to. Hunting dogs frequently show allergic reactions, such as sneezing or running eyes, after a run in the field. Unless the sneezing continues for more than a day, I ignore the whole thing. If the reaction is severe you should get some medicine for the dog's relief.

ACCIDENTS: Any time my dog is hit by a car, even if he gets up and seems to feel fine, I have him checked by the veterinarian. Internal injuries do not always develop immediately.

DIARRHEA: This is such a common complaint that we may overlook the fact that it is dangerous if not checked, especially in puppies. Diarrhea can result from something as simple as a change in diet or an emotional upset. It can also be the symptom of serious illness, such as internal parasites, poisoning or infection. It may even precede the common cold. Whatever the cause, help must be found as soon as possible. If the stools do not return to normal after two days of a bland diet, take the dog to a veterinarian.

FEVER: A warm, dry nose is not a sign of fever. The only accurate way to find out if your dog has a fever is to take its temperature. A normal reading for a dog is about 101 to 102.5 degrees Fahrenheit. Giving aspirin may reduce the temperature, but you should watch for further signs of illness.

If the fever is gone by the second day and the dog is eating well and seems perky, I usually assume that the dog has had a light upset and is now fine. However, if the dog is listless and still has the fever, don't wait any longer. He needs help and medicine.

BAD BREATH: This is a common complaint, especially with older dogs who are having problems with teeth. You should periodically check the dog's teeth and gums thoroughly. If they appear healthy, you need to look elsewhere for the solution.

Quite often, mouth odor originates in the stomach or intestinal tract. The problem could be simple indigestion, and a change of food could stop the odor. If the odor persists, I usually give my dog a little charcoal, available in pet stores. It is supposed to aid digestion. If the problem

persists, try some of the commercial breath sweeteners for dogs. Many times, bad breath is hard to diagnose. If you cannot find the answer within a reasonable time, take your dog to the veterinarian for a good checkup.

SCOOTING: When your dog occasionally drags his bottom across the grass, don't immediately think it needs to be wormed. Although this can be a symptom of worms, the dog might also be cleaning itself.

If your dog does this often, he probably is trying to release excess pressure on anal glands located directly beneath and to each side of the tail. The veterinarian can relieve the problem by evacuating the glands in a few minutes. Don't wait too long as the anal glands may become infected and develop abcesses.

CONVULSIONS: These frightening episodes are always a symptom of some problem. They could be caused by something as simple as an ear infection or as severe as poisoning, distemper, brain damage or heart trouble. A call to the vet is in order.

As a whole, common sense tells us when to go to the veterinarian and when to try a few simple home remedies. When in doubt, a call to the veterinarian may save hours of needless worry.

PROTECTION FROM HEARTWORM

You can hide your dog but it won't help. Heartworm, a comparatively new threat to canines is here and there's only one way to protect your pet—GET A HEARTWORM TEST.

Heartworm is becoming epidemic in many parts of the country. All dogs regardless of age, breed or sex, are susceptible to this threat.

Heartworms are long, thin parasites that lodge in a dog's heart and lungs. If not detected early, this disease may be fatal. Heartworms are carried by the bite of an adult mosquito directly to the animal.

The disease cannot be spread from one dog directly to another. When an infected dog is bitten by a mosquito the insect carries the heartworm larvae to the next canine it bites.

Scientists once thought the disease was confined to warm,

moist areas of the United States. Heartworm disease has now been detected in dogs from the coast of Florida to Minnesota. If even one dog in a neighborhood contracts heartworm, the odds are that many other pets in the area will become infected.

The symptoms of heartworm are harsh coughing, labored breathing, extensive weakness and lack of energy. Many dog owners do not notice these symptoms until heartworm is in advanced stages and is difficult and dangerous to treat.

While cats and humans cannot have heartworm, fox, racoon, bear, and muskrat are known victims.

Since adult heartworm can live in a dog's heart and lungs for up to five years, it is important that your dog be tested each year in the spring to determine if he is carrying the disease. Giving heartworm medicine to a dog, without having the animal tested to see whether he is already infected with heartworm, is dangerous and should never be done.

To test for heartworm, the veterinarian removes a small sample of blood from the dog's leg and examines it for microfilaria. If left unchecked, the microfilaria become infected larvae, which develop into adult heartworm.

When the dog's blood test proves positive, meaning he has heartworm, the doctor prescribes treatment.

When the dog's blood test proves negative, preventive medicine may be started one month after the mosquito season has begun and continued for two months after the season ends. In cold weather states, that means your dog should take heartworm medicine from May through November. Some vets are now recommending year-round preventive medicine for heartworm. However, unless a dog lives entirely out-of-doors, this doesn't seem necessary.

Liquid heartworm medicine is still available and less expensive, but many dogs refuse to accept the taste. Pills are easier to dispense—according to the dog's weight—and do not need to be cut or quartered as formerly done. Our dogs eagerly sit up for the newest chewable medication.

There are other forms of heartworm medicine so it's a good idea to discuss this with your vet and take his/her recommendation.

The cost of the heartworm medicine given to your dog during a complete season will vary according to the pet's weight. For your peace of mind it is money well spent.

COSMETIC SURGERY, AN ACCEPTABLE SOLUTION TO TODAY'S PROBLEMS

My friend Pat has two Basset hounds, each with a delightful personality. One of the hounds had no problems, and was a joy to have in the home. The other spread saliva on everyone, each time she shook her head. The family loved the dog but had always been repelled by the obnoxious drooling.

As the dog grew older, the problem remained. "I felt

guilty every time I pulled away from my drooling pet," said Pat, "and our friends avoided the dog, which though understandable, made us feel sorry for our nice little guy."

Feeling desperate about separating the two dogs and finding a new home for the affectionate but impossible dog to have around, the family consulted their veterinarian.

Minor cosmetic surgery solved the dog's problem. The veterinarian found that one of the deep skin folds at the corner of the canine's mouth prevented the saliva from draining into the throat. The pocket of moisture could only be removed when the dog shook its head.

With a small cut and a few stitches, the pocket was removed by the veterinarian and the delighted family lavished affection on the previously objectionable dog.

As in this case, there are dog owners who find repulsive traits in their dogs after they have grown to near adult size. Deep folds in a dog's skin, which many hounds, Bulldogs, Shar-Peis, and Pekinese have, will collect moisture. When a fold is unable to drain, it becomes infected and quite smelly. The skin folds can be cleaned and the infections treated. However you would have to look at this work as a lifetime task.

CONSULT YOUR VETERINARIAN: With confidence in your veterinarian, a consultation should tell you whether some of the skin in the folds can be removed to make your dog not less attractive but delightfully more liveable.

There have always been cosmetic corrections in the pet world. Eye surgery for Intropin, a genetic defect where the skin grows inward and rubs against the eye, is a necessary and often-used surgical procedure. In this case the operation prevents eventual blindness. And on occasion veterinarians will put braces on canine teeth to correct a bite or for improved appearance.

I am firmly convinced that just as some humans are rebuffed because they are not attractive or have some unacceptable habit, household pets are treated the same way. I am not advocating cosmetic surgery, but you should be aware of its availability if you have a pet you love, but find you cannot live with comfortably.

THE PSYCHOLOGY OF PLAY

Canines will play all of their lives if they are exposed to the joy of fun while growing up. Although most play activity is inherited from one generation to the next, it is an essential action which provides healthy body development and necessary survival techniques.

Puppies, raised with their mother for eight to ten weeks, experience many hours of playful exercise, as well as some firm discipline. The young will learn to tolerate the actions of others, and at this early age, they are already developing the necessary skills needed to handle the diverse experiences they will encounter as they mature.

As the small canine body grows, muscles develop, and bones and internal organs become stronger. Movement and strategy planning are taught and encouraged by the mother as she plays with the siblings.

Each week the growth continues through proper nourishment and adequate physical activity. The brain and all other internal organs then become stimulated and develop, helping the dog mature into an intelligent animal with good health and a happy disposition.

PLAYING WITH YOUR DOG

After a tiring day away from home, throwing balls for your dog to retrieve is probably not your first priority. If you remember how vital exercise is for your dog's well-being, it should give you the incentive to set a scheduled time for play—of course, after you have rushed him out-of-doors to prevent accidental wetting.

During this busy time of day, even a short ten minutes of play and relaxation will:

(1) reassure your pet that you are his best friend and you missed him as much as he missed you,

(2) reward him for being so brave while he guarded your possessions,

(3) allow the dog to jump, run, and enthusiastically get rid of enough energy to allow both of you to settle down and enjoy the evening's activities.

Since dogs find play so appealing, picture your dog's eagerness as he dashes across the park after a ball. To him, it is business. With boundless energy, the hunt is on and the quarry must be returned. Just this one chase has helped to fine tune your dog's motor skills and coordination and improved his muscles and cardiovascular endurance. In fact, lack of exercise can make your dog frustrated and downright destructive.

Choosing at least fifteen minutes a day for fun and games with your dog is as essential for your health, as it is for your pet's. Not only does play between pet and owner form a strong bond between you, it gives essential health benefits to both animal and human.

While your dog was receiving so many benefits from play, you began to relax and unwind from your busy day. Your pulse slowed a little as your body relaxed. You may suddenly have realized the headache that bothered you all day had disappeared. The stretching and pulling of your muscles, while throwing the ball and chasing the dog,

brought a sudden rush of energy to your body and brain—
and—*hooray for play, you feel good again.*

FRISBEE, CATCH AND FETCH

By nature almost all dogs will chase any moving object
if it looks interesting. If you have taught your pup to chase
a ball, the transition to chasing a Frisbee disc will be easy
for both of you.

Start by rolling the disc along the ground and encourage
the pup to run and retrieve it. It won't take long before
your dog will happily bring the rolling disc back to show
you how smart he is. If by chance your dog runs away
with the Frisbee, tie a long rope to the dog's collar to pull
him toward you after he picks up the disc. He must
understand that the game involves both of you and the
Frisbee must be returned.

Once your dog is returning with the disc, you are ready for the next step in this fun game—teaching your dog to jump for the disc. With enthusiasm and energy hold the disc firmly in your hand and move it high and low as you pivot and tease your dog to take the toy from you. This movement will excite the dog and soon he will jump as he reaches for the Frisbee.

As soon as the dog moves toward the disc, lift it a foot or so above the dog's head and say "up." Within a short time the dog will be reaching, leaping and twisting to get the new toy. As he leaps for the Frisbee, allow your dog to snatch the disc from your hand. Praise your dog, but firmly insist that he release the disc immediately.

Another exercise that will build added interest for your dog involves two Frisbee throwers wafting the disc back and forth over your dog's head. This much fun and excitement will entice almost any dog to play the game. Soon you will all be happily leaping with the disc as you share the fun.

From then on it's all pleasure, as thrower and catcher practice daily. Muscles are strengthened and endurance is lengthened. Dog and owner become an agile duo as they leap, swoop, dive, spring and pirouette in a lively game of Frisbee.

THE BEST GAMES FOR YOU AND YOUR DOG

As a pet owner, you should choose a variety of games that are of benefit for both you and your dog. Throwing a flying disc may be just the game for your dog, but consider the activity. Is it safe and comfortable for you? On the other hand, if your dog is very small, perhaps a game of tug-o-war is just the kind of fun he loves. In fact, tug-o-war is a fun game for every dog.

I have often used small foam balls for my pups and small dogs, but being cautious from experience, I cover the balls with nylon cut from a discarded stocking. I can then be sure the pets will not choke on a pulled-off piece of foam.

Tennis balls are probably the best all round choice for ball games. Nearly every dog will race with boundless energy to catch this high-bouncing sphere. And even though they get soiled and ripped, the cost is reasonable and the balls last a long time.

Frequently, I find tennis balls three to a tin that are reduced in price because they are imperfects. Whatever type of ball you use, life is certainly easier when you have four to six balls around the house. With more balls available, my dogs are usually smart enough to find at least one.

Above all, choose toys that suit your pet's size and environment. A soccer ball kicked around the park would be heaven for a large dog to chase, while a medium-sized canine would probably prefer rolling a softball.

Innovative is the word for dog people. I have a friend who raises Bull Mastiffs. They are excellent show dogs and their muscles ripple tightly across their chests, just as good show mastiff's muscles should. Wondering how they were kept in such good condition, I dropped by my friend's kennel one day, only to be told that she was out in the field. Upon finding the group, I was amazed to see two male mastiffs happily pushing bowling balls up and down some small hills.

If you cannot find a solution to your dog's problem, you need help. Consult on experienced dog trainer.

Part 4

Man and Dog:
Living, Loving and Coping

HOW DOG GOT ITS WET NOSE

When Noah was 600 years old, God said to him: "Take your wife, your sons and their wives, and two of each species of animal on earth, and lead them into the Ark." Noah led his animals two by two onto the ship to begin the 40-day vigil. Among the birds and beasts of every species were two dogs (so the story goes).

The rains fell and water covered the earth, a scene frightening to behold. Suddenly the Ark sprang a leak. While man and beast cried with fear, a noble dog solved the problem by sticking his nose in the hole, thus saving the Ark and its inhabitants.

And the Lord said: "Fearless dog, for evermore shall you have a cold wet nose, that no man shall forget what you have done this day."

TWO OWNERS—ONE DOG—A SHARED EXPERIENCE

Owning pets in today's world is not easy. In fact, many pet lovers long to own a dog, but their business and social lives are not compatible with animal care.

There is a solution to this problem—shared pet ownership. It really does work, if proper planning is done before the puppy is introduced into its two homes.

It can be a wonderful option for working singles or

couples who need their free time for leisure or unexpected responsibilities.

Business travelers and retirees can have the best of both worlds while away from home, knowing their little pet is lovingly cared for during their absence.

It's not even necessary that the owners be close friends. In fact, I have seen two strangers with a common love for animals become partners as they successfully co-owned a pet.

I had shared one of my dogs with a relative for many years before I realized that any two compatible adults can achieve the same results.

CONCERN FOR YOUR PET: Sharing one dog can solve many problems. You will no longer feel guilty about leaving your pet in a kennel. You will no longer need to worry about the anxiety your pet feels when left alone too long. You will not be constantly trying to compensate your dog with quality time when you know deep inside, a short amount of time spent with your dog, whether quality or not, is not enough.

FOOD, EXERCISE, SLEEP: Once the dog for duo-ownership is decided upon, a schedule must be worked out between the owners. It should include simple food which is easily purchased near each home. It is important that the pet is fed the same food and the same quantity at approximately the same time in both homes.

The owners must agree to be careful when giving snacks, since no one needs a fat dog.

Schedules for walking and sleeping should be determined by the owners, so consistent habits are established in both homes. This may mean rearranging your schedule for the time your puppy is with you, but don't forget, your responsibilities will change as your partner takes over the care.

DISCIPLINE: It must be clearly understood by each participant that training and discipline are vital to the success of your arrangement. There are pet consultants or obedience instructors who can work up a simple chart for training the pup. All you need do is decide between yourselves how it is to be accomplished.

HEALTH RECORDS: A medical record must be kept and if possible attached to the bottom of the dog's carrying case to be with the pet at all times. Your veterinarian will be happy to help you keep the pup's health record up to date. Of course, the dog must visit the same doctor each time for consistency and the convenience of both pet and partners. Since you will be sharing the medical bills, each partner will be well-acquainted with the dog's health.

WHEN THE UNEXPECTED HAPPENS: It is important from the start that each of the co-owners must remain flexible and realize that emergencies and other situations will arise which could not have been anticipated. These occasions must be dealt with at the moment by whomever is available. When both parties are aware of this, common sense and mutual affection for your dog should help you both reach the right decisions.

CASES AND CAGES

I have always taught my pups that their carrying case is their private property. It is a place for storing much loved toys and, of course, a comfortable place to sleep. Most dogs and cats love their own room and will go in frequently during the day to hide a toy or take a nap. At night in either home, no matter where it is placed, the case is always your pet's good old home.

The carrying case is a perfect arrangement for transporting small to middle-sized pets. It will fit into almost any car back seat, can be taken on a train, and generally is a great convenience for the owners. Should you find you must board your dog occasionally, many boarding kennels will allow pets to bring their small cages with them so they feel comfortable in their home away from home.

HAPPY IS THE DOG WHOSE OWNER LOVES TO JOG

A good hard run is the ultimate joy for any healthy canine. While no jogger expects a dog the size of a dachshund or smaller to keep up with an experienced runner, most dogs from beagle size up will participate in jogging with happy abandonment.

Just as you and I should follow an intelligent exercise program to get in shape before jogging, all owners should be encouraged to use a similar system to get their dogs in shape for strenuous running.

Just as you need to stretch and develop your leg muscles so will your dog. If you start with short runs and gradually increase the length and duration, the pads on your dog's feet will toughen and prevent damage from unexpected obstacles on the paths.

As any jogger knows, food should never be eaten in large amounts before vigorous exercising. This also is true for your dog. If your pet is too hungry to wait, a small amount of food may be given up to an hour before you run.

While running, if you notice your dog is getting overly tired, stop and rest. Remember, the average dog will cover at least three times the area you run, simply because it will trot ahead, to the side, and return many times during your jog.

Certainly no dog should be out of doors without adequate identification tags. Be sure your dog's collar is comfortable and the tags are securely fastened. Attach tags carefully so they will not bump against the dog's body while running.

Under the best circumstances, even a well-trained dog may occasionally encounter trouble while jogging. Be prepared for heavy traffic, other animals and sudden emergencies by tying a lightweight nylon cord to the collar. Wrap the cord loosely around the dog's neck and fasten to the collar again firmly. You should be able to find tough, thin cord that is lightweight, strong and comfortable for your dog to wear as an emergency leash. In case of need, untie the outer knot and your pet is instantly on leash, safe and under control.

Upon returning from a hard run, allow your dog to cool down before you offer drinking water. Gulping large amounts of water can easily upset your canine's stomach. Professional dog handlers frequently give their dogs a couple of ice cubes instead of water. The dogs find licking and chewing ice fun and refreshing, and this small amount of water will not chill the stomach.

As hunters know (and joggers should), dogs must not be fed for at least two hours after a hard physical workout. Larger dogs, or even small dogs with broad chests, may develop stomach gases, called gastric torsion, if fed too soon. It can be fatal.

As a last precaution after your run, when you finish rubbing your own hot and tired feet, give your pal's pads a check for cuts and bruises.

Now both of you get a good rest, eat a well-balanced

nutritious meal and enjoy that marvelous feeling of good physical health.

The reason a dog has so many friends—he wags his tail instead of his tongue.

JOGGING—HOW TO COPE WITH STRAY DOGS

Whether jogging in a park or along a road, coping with stray dogs is a runner's main concern. Most of these dogs are owned by careless, indifferent individuals who refuse to assume the obligations of good pet ownership. It becomes a problem for everyone in the community when people refuse to keep their dogs at home and under control at all times.

149

What can joggers or walkers in a public area do when encountering a strange dog? Certainly they must proceed with caution. If the dog's owner is near, they are justified in insisting that the owner get the dog under control. If the dog is alone, it is best to avoid contact unless it indicates friendliness.

Observe an approaching dog. If the ears are up and the tail is wagging, it is probably just saying hello. Be careful if the dog's head is held low with ears flattened against the head. It is dangerous and you should be extremely cautious.

When faced by a menacing dog stay calm, make no sudden movements and speak softly. Slowly back away from the dog and remember not to turn your back on it. Do not make eye contact as this is a challenge to the dog. Occasionally a dog will growl with every movement made. In this instance, if you stay still, the dog will tire and eventually leave.

If attacked, cross your arms in front of your face and try to remain on your feet. If you do get knocked down, fall on your knees, pull the knees to your chest and try not to move. This is a sign of submission and the dog may stop attacking and declare himself the winner.

Dogs love to chase moving things. It's their natural instinct. If you are on a bicycle and a dog chases you, think fast. If you cannot get away from the dog, dismount, keeping the bike between you and the dog.

Never tease, chase or corner an animal. It may attack because it is afraid and cannot escape.

Ninety percent of the dogs that roam are friendly and want to play. However, there is always a chance that a hostile dog may come near some one in your family. The best way to protect children is to teach them safety rules and warn them not to approach any dog they do not know.

DOMESTIC AND OVERSEAS TRAVELING

Taking your dog along when you travel can be an enjoyable experience. It is definitely cheaper than boarding your pet and you can have a carefree vacation knowing that your best friend is well-cared-for as he travels each day with you.

While planning your trip, write ahead for free directories which list hotels and motels that allow dogs to stay with you in your room. For this information consult the American Automobile Association, the Mobil Travel Guide, or any major hotel chain directory. When cruising, you will find there are ships which will include your pet at an additional cost.

When traveling in a large city in the United States, assume that your dog won't be allowed into zoos, funlands, museums, theaters or restaurants. On the other hand, almost all federal parks and recreation areas allow dogs. Many city and state parks, as well as private camping grounds also permit pets. You are required to keep your pets under control at all times. No pets are allowed in wildlife preserves.

MOTOR HOME AND TRAILER TRAVELS: Many of today's travelers prefer to use a motor home, large van, or travel trailer. This is a most convenient way to take your pets along. When traveling in a warm weather area, for both your comfort and your pet's, install a generator in your mobile unit to provide air conditioning. A generator will provide cool air using approximately one/half gallon of gasoline per hour.

GOING ABROAD: If you expect to take your pet abroad with you, advance planning is a must. Consult with the diplomatic consulate you will visit and request a list of regulations for canines entering their country. Many countries have very strict rules for visiting pets. Once you have entered, you will find to your delight that dogs in numerous countries in Europe accompany their owners into restaurants, hotels and even on public transportation.

VACATION SAFETY TIPS

Here are a few suggestions to make this year's vacation both safe and happy for you and your dog.

BE SURE YOUR dog wears a strong collar properly fitted so it cannot accidentally slip off. Rabies and identification tags should be securely attached to the collar.

NO MATTER HOW well-trained your dog is, never let it off the leash while out of doors. It takes only a minute for it to panic and run away. If possible, take along a long rope for the dog's exercise.

NEVER ALLOW YOUR dog to ride in the car with its head out of the window. Dust, dirt, stones and debris may get into the eyes and cause serious damage.

NEVER ALLOW YOUR dog to ride in a pickup truck. Thousands of canines die each year from falling from moving truck beds.

FEED YOUR DOG less while traveling and give it ice cubes to chew instead of allowing it to drink excessive amounts of water. This will reduce the number of rest stops.

WHEN VISITING A HOME with a dog living in it, make arrangements for the dogs to meet on neutral territory, such as a parking lot or park, before taking them into the house. This should prevent fights.

DO NOT EXPECT even the best trained dog to sleep in the basement or garage of a strange home. It is best to tie your dog by a short leash in the same room in which you sleep. Then you both will be content.

Most of all, be a responsible pet owner, and don't allow your dog to misbehave in public. Walk your dog in the fields and try to leave all areas clean. The easiest way to pick up your dog's feces is with a zip-lock bag. You can always have one of these inexpensive bags in your coat pocket as they are small, lightweight, and strong. Turn the bag inside out, slip it over your hand, pick up the dog dirt, pull the bag back over your hand and zip it up. You then have a clean, odorless package, which can be disposed of in any trash container. If we all make an effort to be clean, we will be welcomed by everyone when we travel with our pets.

HOT DIGGITY DOG—BUT NOT IN THE GARDEN

As we browse through our catalogs, dreaming of abundant gardens, we should also remember the pests that every year invade our carefully tended flower and vegetable beds.

Along with the aphids and cutworms comes the biggest pest of all—the beloved family dog. A dog can do more damage to a garden in five minutes of digging than all the bugs can do in an entire summer.

While there is no absolute trick that will make every dog resist digging in the soft, moist, fragrant soil, here are a few suggestions that may encourage your canine pal to find other methods of fun.

154

As a first step, consider using some movable, inexpensive fencing around your freshly planted garden. A foot high fence often will discourage your dog from invading the area you wish to protect. In fact, once the area has some growth, it may no longer appeal to the dog and the fencing can be removed. This method is particularly effective with young dogs.

If your dog is digging in just one area, fill the hole with rocks. Most pets find the rocks uncomfortable to dig into and quickly find something else to do with their bruised paws. For a really persistent dog, fill the holes with rocks, place a piece of chicken wire on the top and cover with a layer of soil. This is quite a surprise to the stubborn digger.

When the weather is dry, there are some excellent dog repellent products which may be purchased in any pet supply shop. However, once it rains, these products are no longer effective and the treatment must be repeated. Large amounts of red or black pepper may be mixed in the soil as a repellent when the weather permits. Pepper also works in sand boxes or plant soil to repel cats.

After you have tried every trick in the books and all have failed, there is only one thing left to do—CATCH YOUR DIGGER IN THE ACT. Yell at him, spray water, shoot a cap gun, or throw a can containing stones that rattle at the dog's feet. Anything goes with this digger. Hitting won't help. The dog will only learn to shy away from your hand. However, you have a right to let your dog know what you will and won't allow in the yard. Your dog will sense your anger and realize his mistake.

Most of all, don't give up when you have a problem. *Remember, you are smarter than your dog.* With a little thought you will find an answer to any training challenge that your dog presents.

INTRODUCING SECOND DOG IS TOUCHY

If you have ever introduced a second dog into your household, you know what a trauma it can be for the established protector of the home and guardian of the family.

Our Shetland Sheepdog Kilty had made it perfectly clear that she wouldn't tolerate intruders, including other dogs, so we followed careful plans for bringing home our new puppy.

156

The system is exactly the same as we have used many times with friend's or relative's visiting dogs. After a call from the breeder, my husband Jim and I went to Hickory Corners to get a 3-month-old Standard Poodle. It was all very exciting, since we had waited many months for the perfect mother to whelp the perfect black female pup in the perfect kennel. All plans were ready for the introduction of the pup named Libra to Kilty, our resident canine dictator.

The conscientious breeder loaded us with instructions on feeding, grooming and preventive shots, then cheerfully waved goodbye.

An hour later we pulled into a service station on the outskirts of our city. While Jim had the car cared for, I called home to let the family know we were in town.

Our son Kelly knew, by pre-arranged plan, exactly what to do. A short time later when we drove into an empty parking lot there sat Kelly with Kilty on her leash beside him.

As we placed the pup on the ground, Kilty gave her a few preliminary sniffs, then a playful swat and the two dogs were playing happily together.

Of course, if you think about it, you know why we went to the bother of introducing the dogs on neutral territory. It was because the older dog felt she could relax and be friendly. There was no need to protect her home and property.

After 15 minutes we put the dogs in the car, drove home and went into the house together.

157

Poor Kilty had been duped again by her human family. However, she graciously consented to help us raise and train her new playmate.

When we brought our new puppy home, we gradually allowed the dogs to enjoy each other's company. We placed Libra in her pen during the day, and when they played together in the evening, we removed the pup if she tired or irritated the older dog.

It was important to have separate dishes of food and water for each dog. One dish of food and one dish of water was kept a good distance from the other two dishes and we always fed both dogs at the same time. Dogs will go from one dish to another, but with two dishes of each, they will not have a reason to fight over their food.

This method usually disappoints the dominant dog who is looking for a good reason to fight. But since it takes two, the agreeable dog will refuse to squabble over its food if another dish is available. Each time we fed young Libra, we gave Kilty a treat. If weight is a problem, one kibble, given lovingly, will do.

If a bossy dog cannot fight over his food, a battle over a toy or bone will do just as well. Because of this, you will be smarter than your dog if you go to the butcher shop and get two knuckle bones for the dogs to chew on. Also buy two tennis balls, and two rawhide chew toys for the dogs to play with.

Jealousy is bound to occur occasionally and it will be absolutely necessary for you to assert yourself as the leader and stop any growling or aggressive behavior as soon as you notice it. A loud, firm "no" yelled at both dogs will stop the aggressor, if you start this training while the larger dog is young.

Probably guarding our home was the most important task that Kilty taught to Libra. Both dogs, though gentle, relentlessly watched that no intruder (especially the trash collector) invaded our home or property.

Though raising two dogs together sounds like a lot of work, it was not much more bother than caring for a single dog. The joy and entertainment we received from living with two playful, affectionate companions more than compensated for any work involved.

FINDING A NEW HOME FOR YOUR PET

Every day people move. Families grow and buy larger houses. Retirees sell family homes and venture off to warmer climates. Separation, divorce and re-marriage change our lifestyle.

Each year over 37 million Americans change their addresses. Even though the move may be happily anticipated by the family, a painful moment comes when they realize that they must find a new home for a beloved pet.

Nothing really relieves the anguish and guilt at this time, but going about it the right way can help both you and your pet.

The first place to look for a new home for your pet is among friends and relatives. These people are familiar with your animal and may feel some affection for it. This eases the transition for the animal, especially an older dog or cat which will have a more difficult time adjusting to new surroundings. Your family will feel less guilty about leaving the animal knowing that the pet is being well cared for by trusted people.

When no friend or relative is available or willing to adopt the pet, it's time to advertise. A notice placed on the bulletin board of the local supermarket or laundromat may bring results. If not, place a classified ad in the newspaper.

Above all, be truthful in your ads. If your pet is not fond of small children, request a home with older people. On the other hand, if the pet has always romped with children, it might be lonesome on an isolated farm with no young people around.

If pets are neutered, there is a greater chance that someone will eagerly accept the animal.

Many people who love their pets, but are forced to get rid of them, are heartbroken at the thought of taking them to the animal shelter. The staffs at the shelters understand the concern an owner feels when leaving a much-loved pet. Many shelters suggest that you leave a notice on the shelter's bulletin board with your telephone number, so interested parties can contact you. You can then keep the pet at home while you wait. In some shelters you can call and tell the breed, age and general description of your dog and you will be called if the pet is placed.

Placing an older pet in a new environment sometimes is too cruel. Generally, any cat or dog 10 to 15 years old will have a difficult time adjusting to a new situation unless it is in the house of someone the animal knows and loves. Rather than force an old pet to make too strenuous a change, it may be best to have the beloved friend gently and painlessly put to sleep. It is a difficult decision to make and only you, the owner, knows what is best for your pet.

Regardless of how the situation is handled, getting rid of a pet is unpleasant. We should all think of this before bringing another animal into our home and hearts. Being sure that we are able to provide a safe, comfortable home for the lifetime of the pet will save all concerned a great deal of frustration and heartache.

A DAY IN THE LIFE OF LASSIE

Wakes up
stretches and scratches
eats breakfast
teaches an illiterate to read and write
feeds the hungry of the world
saves sixty children from a flaming orphanage
frees the slaves
delivers a baby in the back seat of a cab
makes America safe for democracy
sniffs a couple fireplugs
takes a nap 'til lunchtime.

ALFRED J. BRUEY

162

Index

Abcesses, 129
Accidents, 127
Adult dog
  isolated, 75-77
  retraining, 73-77
  wetting, irresponsible, 106-107
Allergies, 126-127
Alum, 76
Ammonia, 21
Anal glands, 129
Anemia, 113, 126
Auto riding, 44-48, 50, 151-153

Baby, new in home, 105-106
Ball games, 26-29, 32-33,
  42-43, 139-140
Balloons
  deterrent use, 79-80
  training with, 77-80
Barking
  control of, 16, 98-101

muzzle holding, 100
watchdog, 88, 99, 101
Bath
  ear care, 118, 121-124
  eye care, 118
  tub shampoo, 117-119
Behavior problems, see
  Discipline
Biting
  fear symptoms, 8-9
  house pets, by, 7-8
  protection from, 10-11
  puppy training, 7-11
  severe treatment for, 62
  snapping, 10, 14, 62, 69
Bladder problems, 104-105
Brain damage, 130
Breath
  bad odor, 128-129
  breathing difficulty, 126, 131
  brushing, 117

Carrying cases/cages, 146
Castration, 65
Chewing
    destructive behavior, 22-24,
        75-77
    deterrents, 12-13, 24, 74-76
    leashes, 36
    older dog discipline, 75-77
    teeth care, 22-23
    wood, 12, 23-24
Cold, common, 128
Collar
    bolting control, 85-87
    chain link, 35-36, 60
    fashionable/practical, 34-36
    flea, 112-116
    heeling lessons, 37-39
    identification tags, 147-148,
        152
    jerking for obedience, 60, 62,
        99-100
    obedience class use, 69
    rope injury, 18
    skin rash, 116
    traveling, while, 152
"Come when called" lesson,
    26-31, 84-85
Commands
    consistent use of, 41-44, 99
    emphasized, 48-49
    ignoring previously obeyed,
        104-107
    obeying, 26-33, 58-61, 92-98
    timing of, 48-49
    trainer's use of, 68-70
Communication, man/dog, 58-60
Confinement
    area/room, in an, 12-16, 50
    basement, 14, 153
    collar, see Leash

disciplinary actions, 75-77
    evening training, 17-19
    garage, 14, 153
Convulsions, 116, 129-130
Cosmetic surgery, 132-134
Coughing, 127, 131
Cruelty, 59

Depression, 3-4
Diarrhea, 116, 128
Digging, 7, 154-156
Discipline, see specific problem
    balloons, training with, 77-80
    behavior, destructive, 7
    calling to come, 26-28, 84-85
    consistent use of, 22, 99, 107
    duo-ownership rules, 143-146
    food possessiveness, 52
    hitting, as a, 21, 28
    hold to prevent injury, 9-11, 53
    mother dog's training, 9
    newspaper, rolled, 53
    overdone, 53
    snapping the nose, 99-100
    tolerance teaching, 9
Distemper, 130

Ears
    bathing, 118, 121-122
    care of, 121-124
Emotional problems, 104-107
    loneliness, 15-17, 52-53
Enclosures, see Confinement
Energy, lack of, 131
Environment
    change in, 3, 9, 106, 161
    loving, fun-filled, 44
    out of doors, 14
Exercise
    breathing difficulty, 51, 126

Exercise (*cont.*)
  duo-ownership rules, 144-146
  heat of day, 50-51
  jogging program, 147-151
  playtime schedule, 134-136
Eyes
  bathing, 118
  cosmetic surgery, 133-134
  runny, 126-127
  sight, 4

Family responsibility
  attitude, owner's, 3-5, 16-19,
    51-54, 58-60, 75-77, 101
  barking control, 98-101
  duo-ownership of one dog,
    143-146
  feeding, 16-17, 52
  handling, 11
  home, finding new, 160-161
  humans smarter than dogs,
    87, 156
  leadership, 101
  playtime schedule, 134-136
  traveling, while, 151-153
Feces
  clean-up, 153
  evacuating, 129
Fever, 51, 128
Fighting, control of, 158-159
Flea, collar/control of, 112-116
Food
  appetite, 52
  blackmail, used as, 26
  diarrhea, 128
  duo-ownership rules, 144
  feeding dish/bowl, 12, 52,
    158-159
  fussy eater, 52
  kibbles, 52, 83

lunch schedule, 16-17
overweight, 3, 50
possessiveness, 52, 158-159
refusing, 106
stealing, 74
stomach gas, from, 148
tidbits as rewards, 6, 28, 30,
  45, 74-75, 83, 88, 102-104
traveling, while, 153
trick, balance on nose,
  101-104

Games, see *Toys*
Garden damage, 154-156
Growling, food possession,
  52, 159

Health records, duo-ownership,
  145-146
Heart trouble, 130
Heartworm
  breathing difficulty, 126
  test for, 130-131
  worms, scooting relief, 129
Heat
  exhaustion/stroke, 49-51
  female, (in), 63-66
Heeling on leash, 37-38
Holding
  injury prevention, 9-11, 53
  nipping protection, 9-11
  puppy, 9-11
Home, see *Environment*
Housebreaking, see *Wetting*

Injury
  internal, 126-127
  prevention out-of-doors, 14
  puppy, hold to prevent, 9-11,
    53

Injury (*cont.*)
    rope confinement, 17-19
    traveling, open window, 153
Isolation, see *Loneliness*
    all day, 15-19
    chewing discipline, 74-77
    destructive behavior, 7, 14
    learning disadvantage, 41
    older dog, 75-77

Jealousy
    aggressive behavior, 158-159
    neutral territory, meeting on,
        153, 156-159
    new baby/kitten, 105-106
    second dog, 156-159
Jogging, 147-151
Jumping
    injury prevention, 9-11, 53
    invitation, by, 40-41, 44-45,
        47
    uninvited, 39-40, 78-79, 96

Key words/appropriate action
    dog control, use for, 41-44,
        92-93, 101
    list of, 44
Kidney problems, 104-105

Leash, see *Collar*
    command response, 58-60
    heeling lessons, 37-38
Lessons, associate words with
    action, 41-44, 92, 101
    "bad dog," 77
    "ball," 29, 42-43
    "bye bye," 46
    "carry," 87, 92-95
    "come," 26-33, 84-85
    "down," 60-61

"fetch," 27, 95, 137-138
"give," 28-29, 92-93
"good dog," praise, 41, 43,
    102-103
"heel," 38
"hold," 92-95, 102
"inside," 20
key words, list/use, 41-44,
    92, 101
"no," 10, 16, 40, 48, 53,
    78, 103
"on your rug," 96-98
"out," "outside," 19-21,
    42-43
"play dead," 87
"please," 43
"quiet," 88, 99-100
release from position, "OK,"
    "all right," 31-33, 38,
    41, 46-47, 60, 67, 94, 103
"sit-stay," 31-33, 46, 48,
    60-61
"sit up," 80-83
"sit," wetting control, 67
"speak-say," 87-89
"stay," 37, 97, 102
"take," 92-95
"thank you," 43
"up," 138
"use your paper," 20-22
Lifestyle, changes in, 3-4
Loneliness, see *Isolation*
    absence, family member, 106
    alone, staying, 15-19, 52-53
    desertion, 106
    lunchtime schedule, 16-17
Love, meaning of, 15, 59

Manners, good, 48-49
Massage, 4-5

Memory
  emotional problem, 104-105
  lessons retained, 27
  sex life, 63-66
Mosquito bite, 130-131
Mouth, see *Teeth*
  cosmetic surgery, 132-133
  examination, 10-11
  muzzle control, 99-100
  obstruction, throat, 126-127
  odor, 128-129
Moving, see *Environment*

Nail care, 119-121
Neutering, 53, 65-66, 161
Newspaper
  "carry" lesson, 93-96
  discipline, rolled, 16, 53
  floor covering, 12

Obedience, see *Discipline,*
  Lessons, Tricks
  meaning of, 59
Obedience class
  age to start, 61-62
  graduation trial, 30-31
  handler's attitude, 58-60,
    68-70
  heeling, 37-38, 68-69
  instructors, 30-31, 62-63,
    68-70
  preparing for, 31-33
Ownership shared, 143-146

Parasite
  diarrhea symptom, 128
  ears, 121-123
  heartworm, 130-132
Pepper, red/black, as deterrent
  chewing, 24, 76

garden digging, 155
Permissiveness, meaning of, 59
Plants, poisonous, 90-91
Pneumonia, 127
Poem, Alfred J. Bruey, 162
Poisoning
  convulsions, 129-130
  diarrhea, 128
  flea collar, 115-116
  insecticide/fungicide, 91
  materials swallowed, 22
  plant, 90-91
  veterinarian called, 128
Praise
  discipline, associate with, 28
  immediate, 11
  reward, as, 28, 32-33, 51-53,
    68, 99-100
Puppy training
  age, obedience class, 61-62
  auto riding, 44-48
  bad habits prevented, 6-11
  barking, 98-99
  chewing, 12, 22-24
  communication, 58-60
  first lessons, 9-11, 15-17
  good manners, 48-49
  growing puppy, 16-17
  mother dog's training, 9, 134
  shyness/nervous problems,
    25-26
  staying alone, 15-16
  toilet training, 16-22, 135

Rabies tags, 152
Rash, flea collar
  dog, 116
  human, 116
Rope
  confinement, 52, 60-61, 153

Rope (*cont.*)
  drag rope control, 99-100
  evening training, 17-19
  exercise, 147-149, 152
  Frisbee game, 137-138
  housebreaking, 19, 107
  walking, 29-30, 147-148

Scooting, 129
Second dog, 156-159
Sex life, 53, 63-66, 161
Shelter, animal, 161
Sleep
  area restricted, 61
  bed, 52
  duo-ownership rules, 144
Sneezing, 127
Socialization, 25-26
Spayed female, 53, 63-66, 161
Stories/legends, 26, 57-58,
  111-112, 143
Stray dogs, 79, 149-151

Tabasco sauce, 12, 24, 75-76,
  91
Teeth
  bad breath, 128-129
  chewing/cleaning, 22-23
  cosmetic surgery, 134
Temperature
  bath water, 119
  body, normal, 51
  fever, 51, 128
  heat stroke, 49-51
Toilet training, see *Wetting*
Toys/games
  ball games, 26-28, 31-33,
    138-140
  bowling balls, 140
  Frisbee, 137-138

"King of the Mountain,"
  6
nylon pull toy, 70-73
pen, in a, 16
rawhide chew toys/bones,
  74-75
rotating, 6, 74-75
tennis balls, 139
tug-o-war game, 70-73, 139
Traveling
  domestic, 151-153
  keep cool, while, 49-51
  overseas, 151-152
  plan ahead, 151-152
  training a pet for, 44-48
  vacation tips, 152-153
Tricks
  "carry," "fetch," 92-96
  food balanced on nose,
    101-104
  "sit-up" lesson, 80-83

Urine, smell, 21

Veterinarian
  choosing a, 124-125
  cosmetic surgery, 132-134
  health records, duo-ownership,
    145-146
  illness checks, timing crucial,
    49-51, 126-130
  medicine giving, 131-132
Vinegar, 21, 24, 76
Vocabulary, see *Lessons*
Vomiting, 116, 127

Walking, 37-39, 147-149, 153
Watchdog
  barking, 88, 99
  guarding, 99, 101

Water
    bladder problems, 104-107
    bowl, 12
    ice cubes, 51, 148, 153
Wetting
    clean-up, 21
    emotional problems, 104-107
    housebreaking, 19-22, 67-68
    involuntary, 67-68

irresponsible, 106-107
lunchtime schedule, 16-17
newspaper use, 12
sitting position, 67-68
urine smell, 21
Window view
    house, 5-6
    traveling, while, 153
Worms, see *Heartworm*

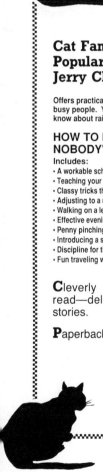